These are transformational devotionals with great depth. Jane offers a fresh and compelling vision of the life of Joseph, but more than rich words, she has coupled biblical truth with practical ways in which to personally walk from famine to feast. There is rich and practical depth in these pages.

—Jo Anne Lyon, General Superintendent, The Wesleyan Church

Finding Your Dream is a lovely journey to the miraculous lives found in the Bible. This is a devotional that is also a study in discipleship, yet it carries readers from famine to feast, telling the story of Joseph in a beautiful, exquisite manner.

—Kathi Macias, award-winning author of more than forty books, including *The Singing Quilt*

Jane Rubietta invites us on a journey through the life of Joseph that will surprise and inspire you. Packed with Scripture and written with personal witness and wisdom, this ninety-one-day adventure calls us to not only understand, but also live in the promise of full, new life.

—Andrea Summers, Director of Ministry for Women, The Wesleyan Church

Jane uses one of my favorite biblical character's life story, Joseph, as a teaching tool to help guide us through the twists and turns of our lives. Life is filled with promises and disappointments; it is how we respond to them that determines whether a life is barren or filled with bounty. Each day we must decide whether we see God's gift of life as tragedy to bemoan or as a treasure to celebrate.

—James E. Swanson, Sr., bishop, The United Methodist Church

What an inspiring journey through the life of Joseph! For every dreamer whose dream has been lost, stolen, delayed, redirected, or on the brink of death, Jane Rubietta's insights will help you dream again—and hang on. You'll not only find your dream in this book; you'll find how it connects with God's heart.

—Chris Tiegreen, author and editor

FINDING YOUR DREAM

FROM FAMINE TO FEAST— THE LIFE OF JOSEPH

Jane Rubietta

wesleyan
PUBLISHING HOUSE
wphstore.com

Copyright © 2015 by Jane Rubietta
Published by Wesleyan Publishing House
Indianapolis, Indiana 46250
Printed in the United States of America
ISBN: 978-0-89827-900-9
ISBN (e-book): 978-0-89827-901-6

Library of Congress Cataloging-in-Publication Data

Rubietta, Jane.
  Finding your dream : from famine to feast--the life of Joseph / Jane Rubietta.
    pages cm
  ISBN 978-0-89827-900-9 (pbk.)
  1. Bible. Genesis, XXX-L--Devotional literature. 2. Joseph Son of Jacob. I. Title.
  BS1235.54.R826 2015
  222'.1106--dc23

                        2014048853

To my amazing husband, Rich, who supported me in this crazy dream of writing from the very beginning. In spite of my late nights, missed getaways, and forgetfulness, your support translates into love in action, chef-dom, and chief barista. I couldn't have dreamt you, but I'm sure glad God did.

Thank you, to all the people who display for me the power of a dream, the power of integrity, the power of a personal walk with the God of the Impossible. Thank you for your encouragement and your hope.

CONTENTS

For free shepherding resources, visit
www.wphresources.com/findingyourdream.

INTRODUCTION

For hundreds of years, perhaps no story has so captivated our collective imaginations as the story of a teen who woke up one morning with a great big dream on his mind. The unfolding of that dream, the difficulties involved in following it, and the costs of faithfulness create the perfect roller-coaster plot for novels and Broadway musicals.

We enter Joseph's story with a bit of wistfulness. Wouldn't it be amazing if . . . ? What if we . . . ? But we dare not follow through on that thought—to imagine that God might speak a dream into our minds and hearts, a dream that would make a difference to the entire world. That's fine for someone in the Bible, but it doesn't happen to us, not in this era.

But all of us long for significance, and *Finding Your Dream* follows Joseph's journey from pit to palace with practical, surprising application for our individual, normal, sometimes boring, usually busy lives. En route, we find that the cast of characters could be our own family, with its imperfect and very human characteristics and dynamics.

More than that, on this journey, God's Word begins to shape us—God's dreams fill our hearts and work their way through us into this world.

When a friend asked Andrew Lloyd Weber to write a little "pop cantata" to be performed at a middle school, no one expected the catchy lyrics, winsome storyline, drama, and picture of redemption that unfolded in the amateur production. Since that 1968 premier, the musical *Joseph and the Amazing Technicolor Dreamcoat* has been performed in over forty thousand amateur and professional productions, charming patrons worldwide.

The musical's journey is, in a way, a reflection of the Joseph story in the Bible. God has far bigger plans than we can imagine, and the musical itself, like the original story in the Bible, awakens our longings to figure into those dreams.

Welcome to *Finding Your Dream: From Famine to Feast— the Life of Joseph*. I am confident that God will prove far bigger than our tiny dreams as we, too, are invited to discover Joseph's life.

To prepare to use *Finding Your Dream*, it will be helpful to read Genesis 30–50 in one sitting, to catch the sweep of story, Joseph's beginnings and backstory, the story's general direction and plot, and an overview of the characters with whom we will live and journey these next three months. Buy yourself a dream journal—a binder or notebook or little bound book—in which to record your impressions and insights, along with God's challenges. Where is God speaking, what are you dreaming, and what hinders you? As we ask ourselves soul questions, we begin to listen more deeply to the answers and to follow God more closely.

Four sections complete each deeper devotion: an opening Scripture, a daily reading, a "Traveling Mercy" benediction, and a one-line "Note to Self." For the opening Scripture, consider reading the few paragraphs that surround those verses, for context and broader understanding and application. The daily reading contains multiple opportunities for potential application and is not intended to be gulped down espresso-style. Take time with the questions and savor the hope intrinsic in each reading in order to maximize the application of God's Word. In our world today, we learn much and apply very little. This renders God's unchanging Word into, well, unfortunately, something that doesn't change us very much. The result, for each of us and for the church at large, is a shallow experience of God's life in us, an encounter much less transforming personally, corporately, and in this world.

We have inherent in each of us a deep longing to hear God speak over us, personally, as a parent might sing a lullaby over a child. Each Traveling Mercy is a benediction, a "saying well," words that God might say to us. Here you'll find words of application, healing, love, and hope. This is where we press our ear to God's chest, in hopes of hearing God's heartbeat for us.

Finally, in Note to Self, imagine a sticky note that you post on your mirror or your calendar: today, don't forget this. Just one thought, a type of application, to carry forward what God's Word offers us.

Ultimately, we find our dream when we find ourselves well and deeply loved, forgiven, and called by God into a life of impact, a life that changes us for the good of others.

It's more than a dream. It's a flat-out miracle.

Thank you for joining me on this journey to deeper devotion. May God open the Word and open the lives of Joseph and his family, inviting us into a dream far beyond anything we could ask or imagine. A journey from famine to feast.

SEPTEMBER DEVOTIONS

DREAM LAND

"In the last days, God says, I will pour out my Spirit on
all people. Your sons and daughters will prophesy, your young
men will see visions, your old men will dream dreams."

—ACTS 2:17

Dreaming: a succession of images forming a story during
a sleep state. Not to be confused with daydreams, small
escapes from daily life where we imagine ourselves elsewhere,
anywhere else but in the tepidness of today. But neither of
these compete with the power of a dream infused by God, the
kind that shapes our hopes and our direction.

Dreams—whether they arrive via our sleeping or waking,
whether sent by angels or by opening our hearts to our hopes
and giftings and longings—fuel our lives and direct our steps
when we apply their impossibility to our limited vision. And
even more so when we invite the God of the impossible to
intercede and interpret and to take us in the right path.

But dreaming, surely, is a luxury of bygone days, those
lazy childhood days that we read about but few of us ever
experienced. And who puts any credence in the dreams of
sleep, all those everything-but-the-kitchen-sink dreams with
random characters and movements and strange, unrelated
scenes. If we remember them when we awaken, we scratch

our heads with a big "Huh?" and go on with our day, the colors and pictures fading like a rainbow when the rain stops falling in front of the sun.

Plus, trying to believe that any dream, whether it came while waking or sleeping, might be from God seems farfetched, vain, and a wee bit loony. These are not dreams we tell others, not if we want to maintain any respect and dignity. Not if we don't want people to consider us arrogant or foolish.

After all, why would we presume that the God of the universe would communicate a heavenly dream or vision to us?

Besides, most of us live our humdrum lives hemmed in by our obligations and our presumed limitations, all the "I couldn't possiblys" that frame our days. The litany of reasons are extensive as to why we absolutely cannot afford to dream: bills must be paid, people might laugh, we might fail. . . . Life is serious and our commitments are real. And then we die.

But to live without dreaming—isn't that a little like dying? Dreams are so connected to hope, hope that life might be different, that *we* might be different, and that we might make a difference. That our presence on this earth really matters in the long run.

So many people live discouraged lives, flattened by storms that lash, battered by disappointment.

Maybe it's time to put on our nightcaps, close our eyes, and invite the God of the impossible to speak into our impossibles. Isn't that what God does? Make the impossible possible?

Anyone entering into the realm of a relationship with God, enters into a world with a history of dreams and interpretations and fallout from dreams and people following dreams. Abraham dreamed, his son dreamed, his grandson dreamed, and generations of prophets dreamed after them. For thousands of years, God spoke through dreams, clear up to the final book of the New Testament, the book of the Revelation to John.

I believe the Holy Spirit still speaks to us through dreams, causing some of our deepest desires to intersect with God's longings for us there in the relaxed land of the unconscious. Where our fences sag and our defenses disappear and the gate to the impossible springs open. Whether we sleep or sleepwalk through life, God plants dreams in our hearts. This leg of our journey, over these next three months, centers around recognizing those dreams, tending them, and inviting them into fruition.

We are never too old, it is never too late, it is not too soon, to dream.

TRAVELING MERCY

Dear one,
Welcome to the place where
Dreams really do come true.
Because when you and I
Dream together,
Anything is possible.
Even those dusty dreams
You've tucked away in the attic
Of your soul.
It's safe here
To dream a little dream,
Or a big dream,
With me.

NOTE TO SELF

Today is a good day to start dreaming.

COMBUSTION OR CREATIVITY

She named him Joseph, and said,
"May the LORD add to me another son."

—GENESIS 30:24

Born to a family of both dreamers and hard workers, Joseph was the eleventh son of Jacob, and the first son of Jacob and Rachel's marriage. They'd waited years and years for Rachel to conceive. Rachel finally gripped her husband's robes and cried, "Give me children, or I'll die" (Gen. 30:1).

The shame of infertility left Rachel in a weak situation. Culture lauded childbirth and scorned the barren woman, whose husband could divorce her if she didn't produce a child. Further, with her fertile sister Leah also married to Jacob, Rachel lived in constant competition and comparison. In those days, it appears Jacob was less of a praying man than he would eventually become, and, as far as Scripture records, he neither prayed with his wife nor offered words of much comfort. In fact, his anger, which, back then, seemed to be kept at a low simmer ready to boil, spoke for him.

"Am I in the place of God, who has kept you from having children?" Jacob asked.

Rachel, in desperation, threw her maid at Jacob (legally, a sort of biblical-times surrogacy), and he and Bilhah had a couple of boys together. After Leah, Leah's maid, and Bilhah, had all conceived time and again in fairly short order, and ten rambunctious boys had arrived, at long last Rachel conceived. After the baby's birth, Rachel heaved a sigh of relief. With joy, she proclaimed, "God has taken away my disgrace" (Gen. 30:23). But she didn't stop on that note. Rather, she named Joseph not for who he was, but what she still wanted. "May the Lord add to me another son," she said.

That seems a bit of a burden to bear through life: a name essentially meaning, "One is not enough; I want another one." Another one would come only after Jacob and family hit the road to return to Beersheba, years later. Ben-Oni, "son of my trouble," would be delivered in such travail that Rachel died in childbirth. Jacob, now with his new name Israel, changed his last-born son's name to Benjamin ("son of my right hand"). He grieved deeply and doted on Joseph and Benjamin, the only two children given birth by the love of his life.

So Joseph, "give me another one," entered the world with the weight of insufficiency already on his infant plate. Because of his father's doting, he became the object of his brothers' derision and animosity. After all, who doesn't want to be the favorite child? Then again, what red-blooded boy likes the favored child?

But the crowning event? Papa Israel created a richly ornamented coat for Joseph to further set him apart from all his brothers as the apple of his father's eye. This went over predictably well, at least, if the goal was further enmity, and that coat became an irritant for the ten big brothers. Every time they saw Joseph — spoiled brat little brother Joseph — wearing that lust-inducing, jealous-making, tailor-made coat, another layer of anger added to their stockpile of ammo. And sure enough, it would only take a glimmer of a spark to get a fire going. And an explosion.

The dynamics (and the dynamite) are set which will propel Joseph into great trials but will eventually lead him into great growth and to a leadership opportunity that most people could only, well, dream of.

Everyone born into a family lands in the middle of both difficulty and opportunity, of disadvantage and possibility. We all enter the world wailing, and less-than-perfect family members inevitably add their fair share of wounds. A little bit of salt and a little bit of rubbing and *voila*! The perfect combination for combustion.

Or for creativity and creation. Our approach determines the difference. The elements for despair, dysfunction, and destruction. Or the active ingredients of a dream.

TRAVELING MERCY

Dear one,
Of course you landed
Smack-dab in the middle
Of imperfect people
Who don't know how to love you
Very well.
But don't despair.
Those are also the people
And possibilities
That lead you to me,
Lead you to hope,
Lead you to dream.
What will it be?
Excuse yourself from growth
Using blame as a weapon?
Or choose to see problems
As stepping-stones
On the way to becoming,
On the way to dreaming,
On the way to really living?
Your choice.
But don't forget—
I dreamed about you
Long before you came to be.
So please choose to be
A dream child.
Choose to dream,
Child.

NOTE TO SELF

Combustion or creativity? No contest.

DO NOT DO NOTHING

When Jacob heard that his daughter
Dinah had been defiled . . . he did nothing.

—GENESIS 34:5

After a warm and fuzzy reunion with his estranged brother Esau, Jacob changed plans at the last minute, rather than following Esau back home as he originally promised. God had ordered the father of twelve (Benjamin hadn't yet arrived as the bookend on the family) to return from Harran. "Go back to the land of your fathers and to your relatives, and I will be with you" (Gen. 31:3).

Jacob reached Canaan, but stopped short of settling near family. We could argue that Shechem was practically home. But we can't overlook the fact that no relatives lived there. Jacob chose to reroute rather than follow God by faith. As unconscionable as this seems to us, we all know how hard it is to trust, and also how difficult it is to know God's leading with 100 percent certainty sometimes. And how easy to rationalize a tiny change of direction.

But this particular decision cost Jacob, his family, and in particular his only daughter, Dinah, far more than anyone would want to pay for disobedience or lack of clarity. In

Shechem Jacob bought the only land he would ever own, and in Shechem the only daughter he would ever have was kidnapped and raped by the village prince. Two of her brothers, Simeon and Levi, exacted vengeance, murdering all the men of the town.

Their desire for justice is appropriate and commendable, but not their method. The death of all the village men is small comfort to a woman raped. She probably wanted that man dead. But the brothers' reaction did not return her innocence or erase her pain.

We never hear of Dinah again. She wasn't marriage-eligible after the rape, and the silence on Jacob's part, his refusal to come to her aid, is appalling. He scolded his two sons for their murderous rampage, and said, "You have brought trouble on me by making me obnoxious to the . . . people living in the land" (34:30). "I and my household will be destroyed." At least the brothers acted on their own belief that Dinah should not have been raped. Jacob's silence was a knife to the young girl's heart.

Welcome to the cold hardness of sexual abuse. The silence, the cover-up, the lack of closure, and thus the lack of possible healing. People remove themselves from the victim and by their silence condemn her. Since Dinah's time, society—and even the church—has continued to ignore or cover up abuse. They have blamed the victims. They have denied the crime. They have perpetuated the abuse by not addressing it. Abusers are rarely brought to justice, leaving them to commit further abuse and leaving the victim without redress.

Grim statistics litter the highway of women's—and men's—souls. One in every six women in the US has been the victim of a completed or attempted rape. Ninety percent of rape victims are women; 10 percent are men. Victims of sexual assault are far more likely to suffer depression and PTSD. They are more likely to abuse alcohol and drugs and to attempt or consider suicide.[1] The effects of abuse last a lifetime, and only with deliberate care and attention do people heal.

In Dinah's case, her brothers went to battle for her, but her father remained silent. Learn how to fight for someone who's been victimized. Learn to be present, to listen and not judge, to be kind, to try to understand. Give the person freedom to talk or to be quiet, but offer support.[2]

The Scriptures remind us to weep with those who weep, to be a voice for the voiceless, to stand up for those who have no support. People experience God's compassion through our ability to love and fight for those wounded in this life. We bear one another's burdens and thus honor the law of God to love our neighbors as ourself (Matt. 19:19).

Maybe you are the victim of such tragedy. Please find the help and healing you deserve. Do it for yourself. Do it for Dinah. Because God stores your tears in a bottle and longs for them to become a healing balm.

TRAVELING MERCY

Dear one,
The pain is great
And the grief, too.
But my specialty is healing the brokenhearted
And binding up their wounds.
I am with you,
And together we will find healing
For you,
For those you love.
You are all precious to me,
And such a thing should not be done.
I am collecting those tears
And will anoint you with them
As you put words to the pain
And give voice to the grief.
Do this for you.
Do this for me.
Do this for all the Dinahs
In the world
Without a voice,
Without an advocate
Without hope.

NOTE TO SELF

Find words for the pain and find help.

NOTES

1. Rape, Abuse & Incest National Network, "Who Are the Victims?" accessed December 30, 2014, https://www.rainn.org/get-information/statistics/sexual-assault-victims.

2. If you or someone you love has been the victim of violence, call the sexual abuse hotline: 1.800.656.HOPE (4673).

LIVING IN TEMPORARY

But Jacob lived in the land of the sojournings of his father.

—GENESIS 37:1 (NET NOTE)

Any paragraph that begins with the word *but* forces us to look before it for contrast. And in this opening for the account of Jacob, which is really the account of the rest of his life (he was 108 when Joseph turned seventeen) rather than the first of his life, we find plenty of contrast.

Esau, the brother tricked out of both birthright and blessing, did more than make do. He fared very well. He so prospered that he lived in Seir, so his herds and Jacob's wouldn't compete for food. There he settled into the land, with his many wives and children and grandchildren and great-grandchildren. Forty-three verses in Genesis 36 detail the descendants of Esau and how they lived and settled in the land.

"But Jacob . . ." But Jacob what? But, in contrast to Esau's settling down, Jacob's tent pegs rarely stayed in one place long. His record was a handful of years, not counting the years he spent serving his uncle Laban. He kept digging up his mailbox and planting it somewhere else down the pike. His father sojourned, and Jacob sojourned. The Promised

Land was still a promise waiting to be fulfilled. Though God had given the promise and the land, God hadn't yet given the order to settle down.

Jacob sojourned and during his journey deepened his relationship with God. Moving frequently forces us to not take our locale or our belongings very seriously. Even though settling might be our first instinct, Jacob learned early on that living meant travel, relocation, and a whole lot of packing up and breaking down and unpacking and setting up. Living meant temporary, and maybe that's not all bad.

Temporary forces us to learn contentment wherever we are. Or at least it invites us into the possibility of contentment. It allows us to view the minor or even major inconveniences as just that: inconvenient, not critical or crucial. Like the shower head that trickles instead of gushes. Or the damp basement—surprise!

Temporary lends us a new viewpoint on eternity, which looks more attractive than ever because heaven will be our forever address. The plumbing will work, the windows will open, and the temperature will always be perfect.

Temporary, however, challenges our routine. Establishing a routine at all in the middle of temporary is like hammering a nail in sand and expecting it to stay in place. Finding a place for God to restore our souls, in the midst of temporary, requires even greater diligence than living in the middle of semipermanent. Jacob's relationship with God deepened while he sojourned. This impresses and challenges me. I want to live in the land of temporary with stakes driving deeply into the promises of God in the Scriptures. That requires me to wait, which proves hard on me when the engine revs for the next lap to somewhere. In the land of temporary, I want to set up my internal inbox so I can receive word from God, which means I have to quiet my yapping soul.

Jacob grew during his sojournings. He became a man of great integrity and deep faith. Esau? We don't really know about Esau. We don't see his character arc beyond him getting over being ripped off over inheritance issues (which is still growth). But Jacob? Jacob grew.

TRAVELING MERCY

Dear one,
You will live well
In this land called Temporary,
And you will grow
Because you will learn
To focus
And to deepen
And to quiet your yapping.
You will learn
That today isn't forever,
And inconvenience
Is just another way
To focus on forever
In heaven with me.
But you?
With me.
Now. Tomorrow. Forever.
From temporary
To permanent.

NOTE TO SELF

But me? But me, I _____.

PEOPLE OF THE LIFE

Joseph, a young man of seventeen, was tending the flocks.

—GENESIS 37:2

Seventeen years old and his life hadn't been exactly charmed so far. Joseph wasn't exempt from heartache or disruption. Along with his whole squabbling family, all those mothers, and all the herds and belongings, he'd lived on the lam, running away from his grandfather Laban after years of servitude and Gramps's deception. They'd hiked hundreds of miles in the desert and dwelled in fear of meeting up with Uncle Esau who once threatened to kill Joseph's beloved daddy, Jacob. They'd survived devastation when a village prince brutally assaulted Dinah, Joseph's only sister. His big brothers retaliated with sweeping destruction, which forced the family to flee yet again.

Then his mother Rachel, the light of his father's life, died giving birth to baby Benjamin. If Joseph was the favored son, life sure wasn't much of a dream. So by the time he reached his seventeenth birthday, he'd seen a lot of desert trauma and loss. Even Daddy's awesome coat of favoritism offered zero protection from difficulties.

Life circumstances so rarely read like a fairy tale. Joseph's life, your life, my life. We all sustain significant damage from our journey to today, some of that damage epic and tabloid-worthy, and a lot of it (hopefully, most of it) mundane. Imperfect people, imperfect situations, imperfect world around us. There's no escaping all the imperfect.

The challenge, daily, is to view the imperfect as the perfect setting for God to work in and through us. It's easier to succumb to a situation, to try to duck under the radar of our responsibility to walk forward in the midst of imperfect. Slouching through life in this manner leads to deformity of soul (to say nothing of posture). We become humpbacked with our blame, weighed down by our own choice to not grow through difficulty. Or by our passivity, believing that if life doesn't happen for us the way it seems to happen for others, then so be it. *C'est la vie*, and all that jazz.

Except that's a cop-out. Of course this is a messed-up world with messed-up people. But we are people of the life not the lie—or the incomplete truth, at any rate—that says, "Give in and give up, life is hard and then you die."

People of the life. What does that mean? How do we become people of the life? Especially with our unique set of difficulties and disturbances and disruptions? Besides it's much easier to be people of the incomplete truth, and it takes work to become people of the life, people who move toward life daily.

People of the life choose, in spite of fear, to ask soul-searching questions. We ask even though we might not get a shiny star in the celestial Sunday school chart for our tarnished answers. For starters, we ask ourselves, "When do I prefer to blame others for my life? Why? What am I afraid of if I take responsibility for my life, starting today?" Until we answer those questions, we can't access or address any hopes or dreams we might have buried deep in the soil of our wounded hearts.

Take notes. Write down what stops you from taking responsibility, where blame started, when you've sidestepped growth in favor of stasis, and, alternately, where you've chosen life instead of the disintegration that results from failure to grow.

After all, it isn't as though God doesn't know all this about us already. But still, in spite of us, God watches us, eyes shining with affirmation and hope. And maybe, just maybe, utter the words, "You are my beloved child. I am well pleased with you."

Talk about favored. That's Joseph. That's you and me. MVF: most valued favorite. That should take away our fear of failure and start moving us forward.

TRAVELING MERCY

Dear one,
Life is good,
And then you die.
But meanwhile,
We have lots of dreaming
To do together.
So take a good look
At what's holding you back,
And let's decide together
How to turn difficulties
Into dreams.
It's not too late.
It's not too soon.
Now is just right
To start dreaming.

NOTE TO SELF

People of the life: difficulties lay the
groundwork for dreams.

A TATTLER'S TALE

Joseph . . . was tending the flocks with his brothers . . .
and he brought their father a bad report about them.

—GENESIS 37:2

The young man Joseph, out in the field of Canaan, tended sheep with his half-brothers, all four sons of his father's wives Bilhah and Zilpah. Something didn't suit Joseph about the way Dan, Naphtali, Gad, and Asher handled the family sheepherding business, and Joseph promptly raced in from the pastureland and reported them to his father.

Typically, tattlers have issues with popularity and trust. Joseph already had a heap of problems with his brothers' respect (in fact, they hated him, as Gen. 37:4 puts it bluntly), and telling tales out of school, or out of the field in this case, only added to the brothers' litany of reasons to dislike Joseph.

Maybe Joseph was right in the report he brought his father. Maybe the four brothers really dogged it out in the field that day, losing sheep to wild animals or carelessness or marauding bandits. Maybe that was their pattern, and day after long day the brothers lowered their standards inch by inch until the sheep were raggedy and thin as sticks, shrinking in both numbers and salability. Maybe Joseph had a thousand good reasons to tell on those allegedly shiftless brothers.

But tattlers, again, have issues with popularity and trust, so Joseph could hardly expect repentance from his brothers, or justice, in light of his tales from the front line.

People in leadership walk a thin and taut rope between inviting excellence from comrades and cowtowing to their own desire for acceptance. Leaders don't run popularity contests. They aren't afraid to take a stand for right and good, whether in work ethic or productivity. But Joseph was seventeen, and not everyone is born with the silver baton of leadership in their hands, ready to pen the next best-selling book on management techniques.

So we can give Joseph a little grace about the tattling. But what if tattling was a habit for him? Why didn't his father rein him in and teach him how to handle discord in the field? Maybe he did and that part is omitted from the story for reasons of space or interest or character development.

But that bad report remains in the family dispute blotter, and it evidently fueled the fire of dislike between the brothers and Joseph. They saw no reason to make concessions for his age, to offer allowances to their spoiled kid brother. Possibly, they also saw no reason to change.

Good leaders with dreams to dream and implement learn when to hold their cards close to their chests. They don't have to say everything they think or feel, but can wait until the vision cures within them and the right next step emerges. They can wait until confusion dissipates like mist in the morning sun. They can wait for wisdom to appear or a pattern to emerge in others' behavior. Maybe they seek advice from veterans about how to handle recalcitrant shepherds or check to see what the personnel handbook says. As long as waiting for wisdom doesn't become a reason to excuse shoddy work.

Still, knowing when to hold and when to show, when to zip it and when to report it, requires time and seasoning, and at seventeen, Joseph had little of either on his résumé. Impetuous and darling Joseph ran home and filed his report before the mud dried on his sandals.

Without conflict, we have no story, and our family encounters plenty of conflict en route to dreaming. The irritant factor ratcheted higher in the tents of the brothers. The pearl was about to be ejected from the oyster, half-formed.

TRAVELING MERCY
Dear one,
Half-formed or not,
You're a pearl.
And all the lessons en route
Will prepare you to be
All that I have in mind for you.
Meanwhile,
Bring those tattles and tattlers to me;
The complaint department is open.
And we can see how to handle them
Wisely
Together,
So everyone learns and grows.
And know this:
However hard the way,
You will come forth shining as a jewel
As you choose to keep learning
And keep growing.
It's not hard when you know
You're loved.
So look me in the eyes
And know that
For a fact.

NOTE TO SELF
Complaints go first to God.

PLAYING FAVORITES

Now Israel loved Joseph more than any of his other sons,
because he had been born to him in his old age;
and he made an ornate robe for him.

—GENESIS 37:3

For most of Jacob's family, life seemed less than dreamlike. All the transitions they'd experienced—relocation, trauma, rage, murder, a parent's death, fear of angry relatives, and more—contributed to the potential for a volatile home life. Into these dynamics the narrator drops one particularly salient detail: Joseph was Israel's favored son.

Ouch, for all those brothers who experienced the pain of comparison and obvious rejection. Ouch, for family dysfunction and the possibility of depression, workaholism, anger, and underachievement because the rest of them would never measure up to the chosen child.

Ouch, too, for Joseph, whose undeserved status as most favored left him vulnerable to anger, depression, an expectation of control, and the sense of privilege. He could consider special treatment as his right, rather than a gift.

Given his own background, Israel should have known better than to single out one child over another as his favorite. He grew up in a divided family: his father loved Esau. Big, brawny, hairy, hunter Esau. Esau, the first born. Esau, who would receive the birthright and all accompanying privileges. Hasty Esau with his enormous appetite for life. Rebekah sided with Jacob, who possibly managed the tents and food for all the shepherds out in the fields and apparently loved to cook. The favoritism led to deception and even death threats, shady transactions, and the downward spiral of the family.

So yes, Israel should have known better than to love Joseph more than the other eleven boys. But common sense doesn't always guide a parent's heart, and although he could have learned to control any outward sign of favoritism, he didn't. All the brothers knew it, and if they hadn't figured it out before, by the time a richly ornamented robe appeared for Joseph, the news smeared like an ugly headline over the family.

Fortunately, God is bigger than all of our dysfunction, and in spite of our messed-up states as individuals and families, God still chooses to work through flawed people and systems. This comforts me, when I consider my many mistakes as a parent, child, and human being. Significant and insignificant failings plague us all, but ultimately, we don't have to be bound by our upbringing, our deficits, or others' detrimental actions in our lives. Jacob and Esau patched up their relationship and stood side-by-side when they buried their father, Isaac. Jacob's relationship with God grew as he grew, and he refused to stay stuck in the deceiver mode attributed to him since birth.

So it is for all of us. We get to decide to live beyond the limitations others impose on us. None of us are victims once we decide to become who God intends us to be, rather than who others decided we were, are, or would become.

In fact, it may turn out that our childhood and our unique set of functions and dysfunctions present the perfect dynamic for dreaming, for the coalescing of God's call on us with our growth and our gifts in—and to—this world.

Imagine. Talk about ingenious—our pain, our past, our problems, combined with God's purpose, create the stuff for dreams.

TRAVELING MERCY
Dear one,
It's perfect.
The perfect setup.
All that mix-up in your life,
The big problems,
The huge pains,
Every single difficulty you experience,
Combined with my love for you
Plus my ability to create good from hardship,
Equals a dream.
My dream for you is beyond anything you can see
And will impact this world more than anything
You can imagine.
So hold on.
Do your work.
Begin to be freed
From the past
So we can move together
Into dreaming.

NOTE TO SELF
My past is perfect for who I'm to become.

BREAK OR SHAPE

When his brothers saw that their father loved him more than any
of them, they hated him and could not speak a kind word to him.

—GENESIS 37:4

Kids will be kids, no matter their ages. Even though ten
of Joseph's eleven brothers should have been old enough to
separate their father's preferential treatment from Joseph's
behaviors that arose from mere childishness, age is no guarantee
of emotional maturity. Their reaction seems dramatic. Hatred?
Unable to speak a kind word? Joseph was only seventeen! But
jealousy and insecurity breed hatred. Plus, some of these men
were not known for self-restraint, but rather for their hotheaded and hot-blooded actions.

Reuben, for instance, took advantage of his position as the
firstborn son and, in an open challenge to Israel's headship,
slept with his father's concubine (who was also a legal wife)
Bilhah (see Gen. 35:22). We hear of no reprisal for his act, until
many years later, when the time for doling out the inheritances
and blessings arrived at the end of Israel's life. He disinherited
Reuben from the firstborn's rights.

Before that, after the prince of Shechem fancied Dinah, raped
her, and then wanted to marry her, Dinah's full-blood brothers

Simeon and Levi conceived a wicked plan of retaliation. For the prince to marry Dinah, the brothers insisted on a bride price of the foreskins of all the men in the village. They agreed, almost unbelievably. While the men recovered, Simeon and Levi "took their swords and attacked the unsuspecting city, killing every male" (see Gen. 34). Their compassion for their sister is laudable, but their actions were horrific. After murdering the innocent villagers, they pillaged everything.

Jacob's only recorded response seems mild and his apparent lack of concern for Dinah appalling: "You have brought trouble on me by making me obnoxious to . . . the people living in this land." Worried about his family's safety, and at God's direction, Jacob immediately moved the family. Only on Israel's deathbed do we learn that Simeon and Levi, next in line for the firstborn blessing and inheritance, were both forbidden from receiving it.

So we consider the source anytime we look at people's lives and their actions. People rarely divorce themselves from their circumstances, rarely act unhindered by prejudice or pain. Neither do we, not by nature. But we can learn.

In spite of his brothers' hatred and inability to speak a single kind word to him, Joseph continued to grow into the man God intended. A spoiled kid, yes, but he would soon be forced to separate others' opinions of him from who he was becoming. This will prove to be a significant strength as the story progresses, and for us, as well. As our own story advances, and as the individual thread of each of our lives weaves in and out of others' lives, our thread is strengthened when we separate our identity from others' impressions and treatment of us.

Otherwise, Joseph would never have risen above the petty hatred and unkindness in his home and never overcome what awaited him in the coming years. He'd never have risen to such a position of leadership.

Circumstances can break us or shape us. Our personality may be formed or at least informed by our family and life circumstances, but our identity comes from God's view of us. It's a mighty means of moving toward a dream when we have less than a dream life.

TRAVELING MERCY

Dear one,
The tarnished records—
Yours, others'—
Are in your ledger.
But once you ask me to forgive you
They are blotted from mine.
Part of growing into yourself
Is deciding to live
With my God's-eye view
Of your life and your future
And what I want to do in this world.
Draw your identity from me.
I formed you and know you
And I will help lead you
Into your God-potential.
Your choice.
I hope you'll choose well.

NOTE TO SELF

Circumstances break me or shape me.

NOT A KIND WORD

And [they] could not speak a kind word to him.

—GENESIS 37:4

Hate crimes, bombings, suicide missions, kidnappings, broken treaties, guns in school, children sold for sex trafficking. Has our world forgotten its sense of right and wrong? Where has kindness gone? Brokenhearted families, weeping tears without hope. A broken world, a broken system, a broken society.

Where has kindness gone? In its place is selfishness and the fear of different. Kindness—a kinfolk of respect—has been replaced by jealousy, such a deep-seated but often cleverly disguised emotion. When I am jealous of another's accomplishments or possessions or privileges, I am really saying that one of my deep fears is my own inadequacy. I don't have what it takes to make it in this world. I am the have-not in a world of haves, so I want what you have. Or at least, if I can't have it, you shouldn't either.

And jealousy rooted in fear turns into an avalanche of havoc and destruction in the form of hatred. Jealousy sunk its roots into Eden—Adam and Eve lusting after fruit that wasn't theirs, after power they were never meant to possess. Within one generation, jealousy led to murder.

Joseph's bad report from the pasture about his brothers didn't help their hatred of him, but their hatred started long before that little field trip. I'm not sure people are innately kind. Some are more kind than others, and kindness is contagious, but mostly it needs to be taught. That these young men didn't have anyone teaching them about kind words and about rising above dislikes and jealousies and have-and-have-nots is a sad commentary on the tents of Jacob. But so many of us camp right there with them. And rising above favoritism to actually respect the MVP is a supernatural work, or one born of desperation.

Well, the situation would turn desperate for all the brothers but not for a number of years would it lead to respect. Meanwhile, the dynamics at home could have resulted in nightmares for young Joseph. Without a kind word from his siblings, he could have become a twisted character in a horror movie.

People's kindness to us, or lack of kindness, is their problem. Our task is to choose how to respond without succumbing to the temptation to either be spoiled or hateful. Retaliation and revenge are just other forms of hatred.

In spite of his youth, in spite of his tattling ways, and in spite of any disadvantages this privileged child experienced, the hard path Joseph would walk would ultimately lead to leadership based on respect and kindness.

It all began with a dream: God's dream to create people. God's dream to call apart a people, beginning with Abraham.

God's dream to love and nurture and challenge and invite into relationship a broken people. God's dream, through Abraham, then Isaac, then Jacob—all such fallible men, all leaders with a rap sheet. And now Joseph, with his many brothers and his elaborate cloak of favoritism and the silencing of kindness. Broken people . . . a heavenly dream.

Maybe that's the work-around for the lack of kindness: brokenness, a prerequisite for learning kindness. And it turns out, broken people make the best leaders.

Hope peeks around the corner.

TRAVELING MERCY

Dear one,
I dreamed of you the other day
In eternity past,
And I know
That the only way through
Is brokenness.
Otherwise you won't find
My love,
My provision,
My preparation,
My kindness,
Sufficient.
You will seek fulfillment and power and prestige
Through prejudice and unkindness,
And those never lead to good dreams,
Only nightmares.
So bring your past to me.
Learn kindness,
Learn healing,
And learn to dream.

It all starts with where you are right now
And where you've been
And leads to who you're becoming.
It's a dream job.

NOTE TO SELF

Enroll today for a learning journey.

SOME DREAM

They hated him.

—GENESIS 37:4

Life in the tribe of Israel must have been rambunctious, rowdy, and a little bit rude—even in the women's tents. Imagine three women, all replacement wives: Leah, for instance. Her father, Laban, convinced Jacob to work for him for seven years to earn Rachel for his wife. On the wedding night, Laban pushed his daughter Leah, the firstborn, into the marriage tent where Jacob waited in the thick darkness for Rachel. He discovered the switch the next morning, after consummating the marriage. Leah, always the less-than wife. Less than lovely, less than loved.

And Bilhah, the surrogate for Rachel when her dream of mothering withered after years of waiting and hoping and trying. Bilhah would never have honor as the chosen or loved wife, though the marriage appeared to be legal. Maybe she had more prestige because, though a servant, at least she got to stand in for Rachel the beloved.

And Zilpah, surely a thorn in Leah's side. Zilpah, pressed into service when Leah stopped conceiving for a minute or two, bore two sons for the tribe. And there she was, childhood servant of Leah, and now a competing wife?

A mess. Conflict potential brewing daily along with the campfire coffee pot. Unless they possessed incredible self-control and refused to let hostility enter the tents, they surely spoke a few unkind words. Really, it's no surprise that Joseph's bevy of brothers offered no affirmation for him. And let's talk about the hatred part of the equation. Wouldn't hatred be highly likely in that camp, with three women who are all scorned and unchosen?

We must choose daily to dream and grow beyond our present, beyond the level of our surroundings and colleagues and even the results of our poor choices. No way around this. One friend, a bank teller, asked for prayer that God would help her not sink to the level of gossip and ugliness behind the counter, but rather live kindly and speak good words to the other tellers. Spurring ourselves higher is simply cooperating with God's call on our lives. God has already called us higher—in fact, the actual command is, "Be holy because I, the LORD your God, am holy" (Lev. 19:2).

Talk about a dream job. Talk about difficult. If we really want to dream, if we really want to live above our lowest common denominator, whether that's our work environment, upbringing, current life situation, or fixer-upper relationships, we need help. Just one of the million or so reasons we need God, the God who promised Abraham and Sarah a child. And when Sarah laughed, as in, "You're kidding? How's that gonna happen? Me, at my age, withered womb and all?" God said, "Is anything too hard for the LORD?" (Gen. 18:14).

No one lives in perfection right now. Whether we camp in contentious tents with sniping siblings or a bunch of worrying women, or whether we come from a family that played favorites or played away work days in the field. Nothing is too hard for our God. So we listen to that calling to live higher. We decide daily that it's worth working toward God's hopes and dreams for us. And to believe that nothing is impossible with God. And if God works with us, and God calls us, then, between us, nothing is impossible.

Those are some really good odds when we talk about God-given dreams.

TRAVELING MERCY
Dear one,
You are called—
Called to me,
Called to live higher,
Called to dream.
Dreaming isn't a lost privilege,
But it might be a lost art.
But start here,
Start now,
By deciding to live higher,
By moving toward better,
Every day.
Excellent dreams
Begin with movement
Toward excellence,
Toward kindness,
Toward holiness.
You can't do it alone,
But you can do it
With my help.

Don't forget.
Remember,
Is anything too hard for me?
Nope.
Never has been.
Never will be.

NOTE TO SELF

Don't do it alone, but do it. With God.

HARD KNOCKS

Joseph had a dream, and when he told it to
his brothers, they hated him all the more.

—Genesis 37:5

Joseph tumbled right out of bed, full of seventeen-year-old wonder and perhaps, also, the assumption that his elder siblings would be fascinated to learn of their spoiled brother's dream while they slurped down their cereal and got ready to dash through the tent flap to work.

Maybe, had the dream been a little more uplifting for the whole family, they would have leaped up and down and clapped Joseph on the back. This dream involved them, just not positively. Joseph, silly Joseph, spilled the whole sack of beans right then and there, no censor in place to offer clues or warnings about the right ears or the right time. And had Joseph stopped for a moment to consider the dream's meaning, maybe he'd have met with a better reception.

But the dream involved the brothers all together in the field, binding the sheaves of grain. (Note: Field + Joseph = plenty of fuel for residual anger. They would not have forgotten the negative report Joseph brought back about their work.) Lo and behold! Joseph's sheaf rose up above all the others, and then—his voice rose and broke with excitement, no doubt, right about now—all the brothers' sheaves bowed down to his. The word in the original means "worship," bowing down to the ground in reverance, as to a master.

The implication struck home instantly. "Do you intend to reign over us? Will you actually rule us?" The Hebrew reads, "Ruling, will you rule over us, or reigning, will you reign over us?" This poetic style poses the two questions in synonymous parallelism, and the structure lends double emphasis and leaves no doubt about their reaction: "And they hated him all the more because of his dream and what he had said" (Gen. 37:8).

In spite of their disbelief, perhaps an inkling of fear trickled in their hearts about now. They hated him for two reasons: because of the dream and because of what he said. And Joseph? Why would he think the brothers would accept his leadership voluntarily?

Still, whatever we think about Joseph sharing his dream so impetuously and even prematurely, dreams in the Scriptures were often, if not largely, prophetic, and prophets were expected to tell their dreams out of obedience to God. So however juvenile he might have seemed, Joseph ultimately acted faithfully, even if he jumped the starting gun.

Our dreams are on a different scale than Joseph's. When we consider finding our dream, most of us aren't imagining that God is prophesying to us for others' benefit. But, imagine the impossible possibility that God wants to impact the world through us, that God has given us gifts to enable that impact. We, too, need to listen and begin to speak of our dream, to give credence to it, even as we begin to grow in wisdom about implementing that dream.

But share the dream wisely, in a safe place. Blurt it out in your journal, for instance, and keep praying over it. Perhaps you have a prayer partner you could bring into your confidence who will put the matter to prayer, praying with you and for you. This is wise protective covering, because, like Joseph's eleven brothers, not everyone will honor your dream. And criticism snips sharp shears under the bloom of hope, when it is young and fragile.

Dream. Pray. Share wisely. Keep praying.

TRAVELING MERCY

Dear one,
Is it so hard to believe
That together we impact
The world?
You have gifts,
Talents,
Dreams.
And the package of you
Is just what we need
To make a difference.
So dream
And pray
And find people
Who will honor your dream.
You won't be sorry
Unless you don't
Listen.

NOTE TO SELF

Dream. Pray. Listen. Share.

TALK, TALK, TALK

"Listen to this dream I had."

—GENESIS 37:6

Progress happens when people dare to imagine *different*: a different way of doing something; a different home; a different vocation or avocation; a different route or circle of friends; a different approach to life, learning, parenting, or church.

Dreams gather momentum when we enlarge our personal circle, inviting others to listen to our dreams. (Like Joseph did, buttonholing his brothers and burbling out his dream to them—although he sadly selected the wrong audience.) With others' affirmation and enthusiasm, we gain energy to act on the dream. Without energy, inertia born of fear or complacency or a little bit of both locks our wheels on the tarmac long before we taxi out to fly. Not that we want a bunch of yes-people in our lives, people who nod and clap even though our dream is in its infantile stage, poorly thought out and far from launch-ready. Wise people can see pitfalls and potential, and these we invite into our dream circle. They provide creative boost for our dream.

Also, talking about our dream to others who know dreams, others who have dreamed and acted on those dreams, gives us courage. We can ask them questions: the hows, the whys. We can hear their journey and what they might do differently, what worked or didn't work. Whether their dreams remained grounded or took flight, we learn from them. Asking questions of experts or of other dreamers forces us to overcome pride (We should be able to do this by ourselves, this dream business) and fear (What if they laugh? Or I fail? Or I sound stupid? Or they steal the idea? Or . . .) and brings our dreams out of hiding.

Still, there are disadvantages to talking, as well. For example, over-talking. Talking can drain our dream of creative energy: we use up all our enthusiasm for the project entertaining others in the family room, feeding on their attentiveness (which we interpret as admiration though they might actually feel trapped by our talk-talk-talking), and then the force behind the dream lessens. Like a hose with the spigot turned on and the nozzle closed: when we twist the nozzle open, water shoots out. But that initial burst quickly slows down.

Talking about dreams can substitute for action. Don't you know people who talk a blue streak about their dreams but never move far beyond the first steps of realizing them? If we only talk, we never really risk. And dreams require risk. There's no way around that, and for the talkers, perhaps fear keeps them talking. Once they stop, they must act or reveal their inability to proceed.

Our dreams may remind people that they stopped dreaming or never started. They may shut down your dream or be jealous of it or threatened by it. See what you can learn from that but find someone else to move you forward. Their negative reaction isn't about you or your dream; it's about their own losses. Some people just can't encourage someone else because they're locked in such painful places.

Joseph, impetuous as he might seem, spoke his dream, and it started him on a journey that would literally change the world. Who knows what will happen when we speak our dream?

God knows, and that's good. Because God is the author of dreams that change the world.

TRAVELING MERCY
Dear one,
I never get tired of you talking,
But beware
The overshare,
And beware
Those who stopped dreaming
Or never started.
Love them,
But do not let them speak for you.
Talk to me.
Talk to a few dreamers
And take good notes.
And hold tight.
We're in for a
Brand-new different.

NOTE TO SELF
Beware the overshare.

DREAM A LITTLE . . . OR A LOT

"Your old men will dream dreams."

—JOEL 2:28

In ministry many years and devoted entirely to God's work in this world, my friends Jim and Linda (not their real names) are prolific authors, have spoken around the world, won awards for their work, and started micro-enterprises in underserved countries. Their tireless work should have exempted them from tragedy, but their daughter's diagnosis of a rare and incurable cancer dragged them deeply into grief's caverns. Her death left a family ravaged by the loss of a bright and gifted woman.

Just as Jim and Linda hit a milestone—a day without tears—Jim's doctor suspected a tumor. When I learned this, I started kicking doorframes, pounding my fists on my desk, and griping at God.

But not this mighty couple. No. While they waited for surgery (another physical problem needed to heal before the cancer surgery could be undertaken), they put their heads and hearts together and created a bucket list.

Not a typical bucket list: go see every sight you haven't seen before, bungee jump, take that cruise. This kind of bucket list is fine, too, of course. But their list looked like a heavenly dream sheet. They pulled out projects that had been post-poned for years due to lack of funding, time, or energy. Sensing the urgency, they prioritized the list and started goal-setting and formulated action plans.

Then they talked and wrote to people who could make a difference, to people who believe in dreams and believe in God's work through people. Jim and Linda then began an online campaign to help raise the funding to get the projects out in this world and start making a difference for God's sake. I was floored and so moved that I wept when I learned of their endeavors. Of their hope for a world where people aren't hungry or sick or afraid, a world where people have access to bare necessities. A world infused by God's love through people's hands and gifts. A world of hope.

Jim and Linda, rather than focus on their own wants, so thoroughly love God that they focused on God's wants. Although, maybe that's not the whole of it. Because doesn't the psalmist say, "Take delight in the LORD, and he will give you the desires of your heart" (Ps. 37:4)? For a lifetime they delighted in the Lord, and God's desires became their desires. So when they created their dream sheet, everyone dreamed on the same page.

Well, the prophet Joel foretold it many years ago: "And afterward, I will pour out my Spirit on all people. Your sons and daughters will prophesy, your old men will dream dreams, your young men will see visions" (2:28).

Imagine. Past the age most people retire, and this son and daughter of God just renewed their passports to the land of dreams. That's a cruise of a lifetime.

By the way, Jim's tumor was benign. Enormous, but benign. Now Jim can dance with his wife on that cruise of a lifetime.

TRAVELING MERCY
Dear one,
You're never too old
To start dreaming.
So pull out that list
And we'll pore over it.
And I will pour out my Spirit
And together
We will dream.
Let me cast a vision
For what the world can be—
Where people love one another
Like I love them.
Like I love you.

NOTE TO SELF
Time to renew my passport.

WHEN DREAMS KNOCK

Joseph had a dream.

—GENESIS 37:5

Tattling, spoiled Joseph was considered by Jews to need his comeuppance before he'd be able to carry out a dream. He was cruisin' for a bruisin.' Dreams require TLC—*t*ender *l*oving *c*are along with a round or two of *t*ough *l*ove and *c*onflict—to become reality. Enormous responsibility accompanies a dream. Respecting the process and putting in the time necessary to honor a dream and invest in turning it into reality might take a lifetime for some of us.

Some (rare) people jump into the dream ring and land a knock-out punch in the first round, walking away with the trophy hefted overhead. Occasionally we read of a teen *wunderkind* who fell into a dream and became a millionaire overnight or within the year or developed a possible cure for cancer through a science project in eighth grade.

But most people fight round after round, bouncing off the ropes, mopping blood and sweat from their eyes in their temporarily safe corner, and worrying about "boxer" dementia setting in before winning the dream's fulfillment.

Seventeen with a dream. That's a tall order for anyone, and with Joseph's background and character traits, it's Jack-and-the-beanstalk huge. But we know that his reaction, after his dream-tossed night, was to run downstairs in his jammies and talk about that dream. Whether that was wise is another discussion. Still, he honored the dream right away by giving it voice. And that is wise because it shows he listened. If we don't listen before we rub the sleep from our eyes, we might forget.

Even if we only whisper the dream aloud to God, we respect the dream by listening to it and repeating it for God's safe, listening ears. Something happens cognitively when we verbalize rather than merely think about a dream. Just that whisper to God honors the dreams that land at the stoop of our mind, knocking on the door with a featherweight hand. It's a start toward honor and a tentative beginning to opening the door to the boxing ring and throwing in our hat.

No matter our age, honoring a dream and its possibility requires courage. Disappointment, of course, because we might not be adequate. The possibility of failure, which leaves us not only dreamless, but a little more broken than before. (Don't forget, though, that broken people make good leaders.) Plus, once we attempt to achieve a dream, once we start putting legs to the dream and trying to land a punch or two, hope stands a chance of being destroyed. What if the dream crashes? Or we tank?

For some people, holding on to a dream without ever putting words to it keeps the dream safe and keeps them safe. Dreaming is different from working toward that dream.

Dreaming by itself is fairly safe, although it can make us discontent and crotchety. Sometimes the cranky people we meet are cranky because they never worked toward the dream or were told that dreaming wasn't safe, so they quit.

Don't confuse dreaming with safety. Dreams are high risk as soon as we acknowledge them. We may as well take a battering trying to jump into the ring. But the cost is too high not to listen.

Because when the dream knocks at your door, it just might be God inviting you into the ring.

TRAVELING MERCY

Dear one,
Dreaming isn't just a pastime,
A way to loll away your days
And your boredom,
An exercise of your imagination.
Dreaming is one of the ways
You finally relax your ropes
And let me into the ring
With you.
So drop your guard
And begin to listen deeply
To your dreams,
To your heart cries,
To your hopes.
Then tell me what you hear.
You will never be a failure in my eyes,
So listen up;
I may be trying to tell you something.
Talk to me
And let's see.
Between our dreams—

Mine for you and the ones I give you—
And our doing,
We will make this world
A better place.

NOTE TO SELF

Dreaming is either an exercise in futility or faith.
My choice.

KEEPING THE MATTER IN MIND

Then he had another dream, and he told it to his brothers.

—GENESIS 37:9

Just when we think Joseph can skate out of the friction, God gave him another dream, reinforcement for the first one. He went immediately to his brothers and regaled them with the updated version.

"Listen," he said, "I had another dream, and this time the sun and moon and eleven stars were bowing down to me." No doubt the menfolk loved this one, with its expanded version of family prostrating themselves to Joseph. That the child in the ornate coat would be so powerful that the sun and moon (the mother and father) would bow down? The sons of Jacob were not buying into that plan.

Then the favored son ran to his father and told him. Jacob might be the only possibly receptive audience we could imagine, given his own God-given dreams as a younger man. But even Jacob rebuked the boy, incredulous: "What is this dream you had? Will your mother and I and your brothers actually come and bow down to the ground before you?" (Gen. 37:10).

Joseph's answers to his brothers' hatred and jealousy are not recorded. Maybe his self-control peeked through there, because if there had been a brawl, we might know about it. The Bible isn't shy about pointing out the fights in the Scriptures.

The brothers were jealous of Joseph, on top of hating him and being unable to say a kind word to him. But even though Jacob rebuked his son, Genesis 37:11 says, "His father kept the matter in mind."

Jacob, who stole the birthright and inherited the blessing (see Gen. 25:29–34 and 27:27–29), was the son recognized for his spiritual leadership and given the responsibility of overseeing the family both physically and spiritually. With the same blessings to bestow, he would surely be watching over his twelve sons. Though both birthright and blessing were expected to go to the firstborn son, this hadn't been the case for Jacob growing up. And it would not be the case for his sons.

Naturally, then, he watched for leadership potential in his children. Both for leadership of the estate and spiritual leadership. Of course he "kept the matter in mind."

Maybe your parents didn't honor your dreams, keeping them in mind while observing your life and actions and personality. Not all parents are good at paying close attention or even recognizing significant mile markers on their children's journeys. And some kids have so many dreams, the parents don't know what to do with all of them and can hardly keep the current dream in mind. Most parents are doing the best they can with the equipment and training they've received.

But God keeps the matter in mind, God watches over us all, and God invites us into the greatest dream ever.

That the God of the universe—the God who created all things and through whom all things hold together—that this God would call to us and invite us to become family? That God would bestow on us the name "child of God" (see 1 John 3:1)? Would love us with a love that endures forever (see Ps. 118:1–4)? Would promise that, even though our mother and father forsake us, God will never abandon us but will receive us (see Ps. 27:10)? That's more than a dream. It's a flat-out miracle, and the very definition of grace. Divine, unmerited favor and assistance.

TRAVELING MERCY

Dear one,
I dreamed of you
Before time began,
And always have time
To listen to your dreams.
But I do want you
To listen to me,
Because when you do all the talking
And none of the listening,
It stunts your growth.
So listen up:
I can't dream of anyone
I would love more than you.
I hope you will keep
The matter in mind.
And in heart.

NOTE TO SELF

God succeeds even if—when—parents fail.

A READY RESPONSE

"Here am I," [Joseph said.]
GENESIS 37:13 (KJV)

After the second dream-telling, the eleven brothers headed off to graze the sheep, guiding them nearly fifty miles to Shechem. Given the fairly recent history of Jacob's family at Shechem (see Gen. 34), this seems courageous or perhaps desperate. Sheep need to eat, obviously, and if they don't, they die. Obviously. And with them goes the family's livelihood as well as its food. So the brothers moved the flock where they could find grass, maybe a four- or five-day walk if one isn't stopping to nibble grass and grains along the way. Or if a few hundred or thousand sheep aren't stopping and chomping.

Israel called Joseph to his side sometime after the brothers left. "As you know, your brothers are grazing the flocks near Shechem. Come, I am going to send you to them." (Interesting that the Scriptures call him Israel here, rather than Jacob. Israel, the leader, the spiritual head of the household. Israel, the man through whom the promise from God descended.)

"Very well," the NIV renders Joseph's response. We might read it as resignation or the deep sigh of a spoiled child being put upon yet again. But the word in the original language goes deeper.

This is the same word in Hebrew that Abraham used when God told him to take his son, his only son, to be sacrificed. Early one morning, Abraham heard his name, spoken by that voice he knew without doubt, and Abraham answered, "Here I am. I'm ready. Whatever you say." *Hinneni*. Abraham showed up, ready to obey, even though he had no idea why God called.

"Whatever you say!" What a response for both Abraham, being asked to give up the dearest person in his life, and Joseph, being asked to track down eleven jealous brothers who hate him and cannot scramble about for a kind word to speak to him. Would we respond the way they did?

Maybe we don't often hear our names on God's lips, hear God calling in the night or the day either. Maybe the idea of God personally inviting us into a challenge and an opportunity seems preposterous. Not to mention frightening. Look at what God expected of Abraham, after all. And if we've peeked ahead in the story of Joseph, this "Here am I" would change the trajectory of his life. It would become more than an extended field trip to check on his brothers.

Maybe he wouldn't have responded if he could have seen the next thirteen years of his life. Since when, however, do we know what happens next in our own lives? No one knows the future, although we make plans to move forward into the next day and week and year and decade, and figure out how to cover our responsibilities and our people en route.

The Scriptures tell us that God calls us by name, whether we hear God's voice or not (see Isa. 41:3). Every single day we wake up means that God has called us to one more day, to one more opportunity and challenge to show up, like Joseph and like Abraham, and say, "Here I am. I am ready." And even if my life looks like getting dressed and getting my coffee and getting out the door to work, to say "Here I am" to God makes far more sense than trying to get through any day on my own agenda and steam.

So today, say it with me: "Here I am." And the amazing good news is that where we are, God is.

So it's all good. Truly, all good.

TRAVELING MERCY
Dear one,
There you are.
And there I am
With you,
Always,
Even through the end
Of the age.
So do not fear,
But every moment you say
"Here I am. I am ready,"
Minute by hour by day by month by year,
I say, with you, "I am here."
We journey together.
So wake up from counting your sheep
And open up to me,
And let's take a walk
Together.

NOTE TO SELF
Here I am. A moment-by-moment decision.

A LITTLE TRANSITION TIME

Then [Israel] sent Joseph off from the Valley of Hebron.

—GENESIS 37:14

Here-I-Am Joseph set out on his several-day journey north to Shechem, certainly mindful of the terror his family inflicted on the village when his mother still lived. Though a child at the time, he couldn't forget the nightmare. Or all the people and possessions his brothers captured and brought back to the tents of their father. And now en route to find his brothers, the dangers of bandits, wild animals, and the unknown lurked everywhere.

In our current era in North America, parents would never send their seventeen-year-old son on a five-day, fifty-mile trek along a trade route alone. In so many places, riding a bike around the block isn't safe, and kids learn about stranger danger as toddlers. We have dead bolts on doors and install security systems; childcare workers must be screened; Amber Alerts broadcast alarm on digital signs along roadways.

But a long walk in the countryside? What an opportunity for Joseph to think through his life, to reflect on the remarkable incidents of the previous few days—his field report about subpar work from his brothers and their hatred of him. And then those dreams. Everyone's disbelief and outright rage at him (and at the dreams, he surely noted to himself as he ambled along). But his father, Israel, knew what it meant to dream, and even though his rebuke smarted, maybe Israel would circle back to the dream. Joseph had no idea what the dream really meant in terms of fulfillment. He likely couldn't imagine his brothers ever literally bowing down to him, couldn't imagine a situation to provoke that reaction, appealing as it might have been, given their constant antagonism.

Yes, a long walk allows time to process our journey, to circle back through our days and our own reactions. What might we have done differently? What did our reaction mean? Where do we need to seek reconciliation? Or offer it? This reflection time, so scarce in our lives, can help us get from Point A to Point B and arrive as changed individuals.

We pack our lives pretty tightly, like canning jars filled to the top and then heat-sealed. We might pop the seal, if there's any contamination inside. Allowing a little transition time—a walk, or a deliberate shifting of focus while commuting from work to home or home to a meeting—helps us arrive at the next point of our journey more present. Sometimes when I head into a meeting full-tilt, racing through a jammed schedule, I forget to stop my mental chase in order to focus—on the person I will meet, on what I know about her and her life journey so far, on her hopes and dreams and relationships. On current events in her life.

Transition time. It's just one more way to train the brain and eliminate strain.

Besides, a simple walk does wonders for blood pressure. It might keep us from popping when the seal is broken on the jar that is our life.

TRAVELING MERCY
Dear one,
Take a short walk
Or a long walk
Or a mental break—
Anything to shift your focus
To who you are,
Where you've been,
And where you hope to go.
Leave a clean trail
And no regrets,
And you will be
Good as new
When you arrive.
Take my hand;
I'm happy to walk alongside you.
In fact, I surround you
Every day,
All day long,
And night, too.

NOTE TO SELF
Transition time: Train the brain; eliminate strain.

AT JUST THE RIGHT TIME

When Joseph arrived at Shechem, a man found
him wandering around in the fields.

—GENESIS 37:14–15

The man found Joseph wandering in a field. Like Little
Bo Peep who'd lost her sheep, Joseph lost his brothers, who
were a lot more intelligent than sheep.

Jewish tradition declares the man was an angel, Gabriel to
be precise, sent to Joseph to direct him further along the path
into God's plan for future salvation and deliverance. Whoever
or whatever he was, he appeared at exactly the right moment.
Timing is everything as far as God is concerned, and your
life and mine would be entirely different if not for the split-
second exactness of God's timing.

Shechem, land of wounds and war, was not a place Joseph
needed to stay for long. But how easy would it be to mosey
through acres of fields and never find the people you sought?
But this man at just the right moment found Joseph. This
man just happened to have intersected with the brothers and
overheard their plans to move toward Dothan.

Nothing "just happens" in the life of someone chosen and
called and loved by God. We just don't always see the intricacies

of timing. At just the right time, someone shows up to direct us. The right phone call, the right question, the right idea.

I grieved recently over a loss my husband experienced many years ago, asking God even now, "Why? Why didn't I get to know him before that loss, why didn't I know that part of him?" I waited with the question, heavy sobs sitting on my chest like brick pavers, grief freshly renewed after a recent transition. Part of the truth crept over me, subtly: had that loss not occurred, my husband's life would have turned an entirely different direction. The enormous possibility that we would never have met made me swallow, my throat tight. Who would I have been had I not met him? My life trajectory would veer on some dog-legged path to destruction I'm afraid.

And even so, I wouldn't have met him had I not auditioned on a dare for a musical in college, meeting the female lead who would down the road become my best friend and roommate. We would challenge one another toward growth in Christ, and end up at a convention of thousands of people, where I would meet my husband. On an escalator, going up.

In heaven one day, we will hear all the stories that grew from split-second decisions in our lives, from supposed chance encounters or remarks. If a college professor hadn't written on a final senior essay, "You are a good writer," would I have had the courage years later to begin forming words for all the unvoiced feelings and thoughts and opinions locked inside? *Shrug*. I don't know. If my high school English teacher hadn't twisted my arm to be on the speech team, would I speak professionally today? *Shrug*. I don't know. But every word from another has the potential to alter our life path.

God will accomplish heavenly purposes, whether I understand the timing or the rationale behind the events in my life. I know that. But imagining that celestial clock and getting to be part of its schedule forces me to my knees in amazement and gratitude. Just the right person, at just the right time. I hope I can be that person for someone else.

TRAVELING MERCY
Dear one,
You think you are wandering
Lost in a field,
But I know where you walk.
That grass grows because
I water it.
And I will send
Just the right person
At just the right time,
With just the right word,
At just the right event.
So trust me in this
And keep watching.
Your life is not random.
You are not random.
You are dearly loved and chosen.
Just the right person
At just the right time.

NOTE TO SELF
Choose good words for the sake of others.

WHAT DO YOU SEEK?

A man found [Joseph] . . . and asked him,
"What are you looking for?"

—Genesis 37:15

The question for Joseph is a question for the ages, and for the sages: "What do you seek?" the man asked. Joseph answered literally: "I'm looking for my brothers." And isn't that a far deeper truth than we might notice at first glance? He was looking for his brothers. Looking for family. Looking for the end of abandonment and the beginning of the acceptance that triumphs over all the pettiness of a group of boys. Triumphs over the inevitable letdowns of people who are meant to love you, support you, consider you wonderful, and challenge you.

Many years earlier, the angel asked Hagar a version of this question: Where have you come from and where are you going? (see Gen. 16:8).

What do you seek, really? Deep down, whether you are entering a job or a relationship, what do you seek? If we walk into every room and ask ourselves, "What do I seek here?" how do we answer? If we enter every relationship with the question, "What do I seek here?" our relationships would be far more straightforward with an honest answer on our part.

Seeking affirmation? Affection? Touch? The acknowledgment of our humanity or presence? Eye contact that tells us, "You exist. I see you. You have value because I see you."

When we begin to recognize that core longing for acceptance that will counteract any residual abandonment issues — and anyone born into this world receives abandonment issues — we get a clearer handle on our relationship needs. Unrealistic needs, too often, because who can be expected to love us the way we seek, other than God? Actually, we can settle that with certainty because the Scriptures affirm this repeatedly. Consider Exodus 15:13: "In your unfailing love you will lead the people you have redeemed. In your strength you will guide them to your holy dwelling." All forty instances of the phrase "unfailing love" in Scripture occur only in the context of *God's* unfailing love. Nowhere else do we find unfailing love.

This, then, frees us to enter rooms and relationships and jobs and church with an entirely different answer to the question, "What am I looking for?" What if we answered that question, deliberately, consciously, and conscientiously, with "I am looking to offer God's loving acceptance in this place, with this person, in this setting." What if? Wouldn't it change our interactions with others? Wouldn't we be less defensive, more apt to reconcile? Wouldn't we be more other-focused and less self-focused?

Maybe we'd be more intent, then, on what God wants to do in this world through us. More decisive about what issues really matter. Because if everywhere we turn, people are asking the same questions: Who will love me? Who will care for me? Who will care that I exist? Then we can answer those questions with: We will. Because God does.

That kind of question-and-answer session will reroute lives.

What are you looking for?

TRAVELING MERCY
Dear one,
My unfailing love surrounds you,
Everywhere you go.
So when you ask the question
Of yourself,
"What am I looking for?"
Look to me for the answer,
And then for the power to love others
Regardless of their failures.
I love them just as unfailingly
As I love you.
But I will choose to love them
Through you.
So answer honestly,
And let's get to work.

NOTE TO SELF
What do I seek?

HIGHWAY ROBBERY

"Here comes this master of dreams!"
—GENESIS 37:19 NET

The Scriptures don't tell us why Israel needed to know how the boys and the bleating sheep fared. Both groups were his concern, of course, but why the urgency right then? Maybe we don't need to know, as long as we retain this principle: God will work his will in us and through us, and the incidents and authorities and meetings in our lives will be some of God's primary vehicles to accomplish those purposes. Experience teaches us that many things get worse before they get better and cost us more than we expected. A simple journey like Joseph's is ripe for challenge. Particularly since he walked into a riled hornets' nest of men.

The man near Shechem kindly directed Joseph to Dothan, another stop on the trade route, about fourteen miles farther northwest. A sixty-four-mile walk in total. Turns out the walk was the safest part of his journey.

The brothers spied Joseph heading their way and groaned. Seeing their brother in that inflammatory coat, that flaming reminder of their lesser-than status, triggered their hatred once again. "Here comes that dreamer!" they said. "Come now, let's kill him and throw him into one of these cisterns and say that a ferocious animal devoured him. Then we'll see what comes of his dreams" (Gen. 37:19–20).

Reuben's name sounds like a Hebrew word for "he has seen my misery," and for the first time we see him attempt to live up to his name. He practically pulled out his hair at the brothers' plan, and begged them, "Let's not take his life. Don't shed any blood. Throw him into this cistern here in the wilderness, but don't lay a hand on him" (Gen. 37:21–22). He may not have liked Joseph any more than the rest of them did, but he knew, perhaps, that bloodshed will work on the perpetrators.

Thankfully, the brothers listened to Reuben. They stripped Joseph of his fabulous coat and threw him into an empty cistern.

And then, Genesis 37:25 says "they sat down to eat their meal." That's more than a little disturbing, with Joseph battered and bruised, ten to thirty feet deep in a limestone cistern and surely hollering for help, and his coat sitting at the brothers' feet like a trophy. How frightening when compassion and grace atrophy to such an extent that the spiritual muscle memory disappears.

But salvation plodded down the road in a camel caravan, Ishmaelites heading south along the trade route to Egypt. Judah at last lived up to his own name, "God be praised," when he recognized the chance to save Joseph's life. "What will we gain if we kill our brother and cover up his blood?" he asked. (Nothing good. Rhetorical question.) "Let's sell him to the Ishmaelites and not lay a hand on him; after all, he is our brother, our own flesh and blood" (see Gen. 37:26–27).

May evil and pain rob us of our appetite rather than our conscience.

TRAVELING MERCY

Dear one,
I'm still here,
Still on duty,
Though life isn't what
You might hope.
But hope sometimes walks
On skinny legs like a camel.
Your job right now is
To trust me,
To keep your heart and soul alive
To the pain of others around you,
And fight against—
Not cooperate with—
Evil.
It's the only way through the difficulties
To the better-and-better things
Coming your way.

NOTE TO SELF

Stay alive and fight the right fight.

THE DANGER OF A DREAM

"Here comes that dreamer! . . . Come now, let's kill him and
throw him into one of these cisterns and say that a fierce animal
devoured him. Then we'll see what comes of his dreams!"

—GENESIS 37:19–20

Pastor Mick (all names have been changed) only lasted three
years in a church where people regularly hire and fire their
shepherds. Admittedly, at the time, neither the apostle Paul nor
Joseph could probably have led this affluent congregation in
LA's northern suburbs. But Mick arrived with buoyancy and
optimism for finding and following God's dream and mission
for that church. Unfortunately, a small but influential group
within the church nudged him out.

Of course, as in the case of Joseph, some dreams are best left
a bit out of focus for the non-dreamers. Did he have to give *all*
of the details? Anyone taking Dream Interpretation 101 at the
junior college could figure out which corn stalks they were in
Joseph's dream (see Gen. 37:5–7). At least Joseph could have
shared his revelation in stages, as his listeners slowly assimilated
the message that God was sending. But which of us can exercise
much self-control when given a divine revelation?

Why were Joseph's brothers so threatened? We can
understand irritation and even extreme jealousy. No one

wants to hear that they're second fiddle, or eleventh for that matter. But to have such a violent response to a dream?

Penny served as organist at her church for fifty-one years, when the new pastor realized that there were quite a few people within the congregation with a variety of musical gifts. Gradually, Pastor Rob invited a clarinet player, then a vocalist, then two young trumpet players to offer "special music" during worship. Shortly thereafter, Penny stopped her pastor and asked, "Do we really need all of this extra music?" Surprised, Rob answered, "Well, I'm trying to create opportunities for everyone to share their gifts in ministry here." Penny complained to the staff-parish relations committee, one person at a time. Most of the parish feared Penny might leave.

What prompted her strong reaction? The pastor's dream posed a real threat. If the front of the sanctuary is a stage, albeit a sacred one, Penny had basked in the solitary spotlight for half a century. No one else dared enter the stage, until now. What if the spotlight shifted and never fixed itself permanently upon the organ bench again? Penny received most of her affirmation from her role as a church musician.

Like Pastor Mick, Rob's job security was in jeopardy, all because he had a dream from God.

Walter Brueggemann explains the reaction on the part of Joseph's brothers and the congregational leaders in the true examples above: "The dream is a way of hoping for a new arrangement very different from the present. Even as a dream, such hope is a threat."[1]

How human to fear losing our place on the canvas if someone else is painting a picture of a new future. But if God is the artist and we are getting a glimpse of God's reality, will anyone really lose?

A dream can get you killed. But the greater danger for us all is to kill the dreamer.

TRAVELING MERCY
Dear one,
Don't be threatened
By another's dream.
My dreams for you and others
And through you and others
Are for good,
Not for evil.
Dreams represent hope
That the world will be different,
But also better.
It's a stage where we all can play
Major roles.
So don't kill the dream
Or the dreamer.
Dream on.

NOTE TO SELF
What frightens or threatens me about dreaming?

NOTE
1. Walter Brueggemann, *Genesis* (Atlanta, John Knox Press, 1982), 302.

SOLD OUT

"What will we gain if we kill our brother . . . ?
Come, let's sell him to the Ishmaelites."

—GENESIS 37:26–27

On his search for his brothers, Joseph traveled through Shechem, the land of deep family wounds, scars still fresh on the skin of the family's soul. We all make similar journeys if we are deliberate: toward the land of deep wounds, not to stay there, but to work through that territory yet another time. It won't be the end of wounds, not this side of heaven, but each pass-through fosters healing. If we are intentional about it.

Who hasn't experienced difficulty if not outright devastation? The only way toward wholeness is to process it, bit by bit, until one day we realize that we don't hurt. The scab has fallen off and we are free again. For now. But the region of Dothan, of course, was just a few miles up the road for Joseph, and there he—and we—will once again meet with pain. It's an inevitable rendezvous, this meeting.

When Joseph headed toward Dothan, obeying his father's orders to check on the rest of the tribe, he never expected the reception he received. The mocking, the ugliness, and then the shocking betrayal. Such things ought not to be, this selling out by people who are supposed to love us. But it happens. This has happened since the exile from Eden, right on the doorstep of perfect, when Cain slew Abel over jealousy.

The brothers saw Joseph and, their dander up and their jealousy thick as pond scum, hatched a plan that would make terrorists dizzy. "Come now, let's kill him and throw him into one of these cisterns" (Gen. 37:19). Reuben and Judah both redirected the initial hate crime. The sale of Joseph into slavery happened without warning. Snatched. Sold. Gone.

Maybe you've been sold out—a confidante broke your trust and ever since, you are confident in no one, you confide in no one. Or parents betrayed you, selling you on the market of their own expediency so you virtually raised yourself. Or parents overlaid their dreams on you so that they could live vicariously through you. It's still a betrayal, however it might appear to be an offer benefitting you.

Sometimes the selling out is severe: child abuse, sexual abuse, emotional abuse, substance abuse, constant fear, or eyewitness to others' violence even if never directed at you. If you grew up in any of these situations, you likely told yourself all sorts of things to get through the day and night. Maybe, since it's all you knew, you thought everyone lived with abuse, with fear.

Not true. Not OK. And now, in the fields of Dothan, in the cistern of your past, now is the day of reckoning. Now is the day to decide that what you were taught was not true and what happened was not OK, and to begin to grieve that selling out. Only when we acknowledge that we, too, have been sold out— whether a friend, family member, boss, teacher, or pastor took the twenty shekels of silver in exchange for us—only then do we begin to move forward with our lives.

For Joseph, that selling out would lead him from cistern to stronghold, from pit to palace, from servant to second-in-command of an entire country. Perspective helps. We would not be who we are, with the innate strengths and experiences that define us, without the selling-out along the path.

God knows the cistern up ahead and the ones behind us. God will deliver us into the next vital stage of our journeys. So we choose to grieve the costs and the losses thus far and then to cooperate with the unknown future. Thankfully, the future is not unknown to God.

TRAVELING MERCY
Dear one,
You've been sold by people you love.
But not by me.
Don't sell out to hatred.
Don't sell yourself to bitterness.
Don't let ugliness own your soul.
I have far bigger plans for you
Than anyone could guess.
So grieve, heal.
Then hold on to the rope and keep climbing.
It's the only way out of the cistern,
Out of the slavery.
Imagine that I am the rope
And the strength in your hands.
Together we pull you up and out and forward.

NOTE TO SELF
Don't sell out myself.

FILL 'ER UP

The cistern was empty; there was no water in it.

—Genesis 37:24

An empty cistern was good for Joseph's sake or he would have drowned. But an empty cistern is bad news if you're sheep, it's summertime, the living is hot and miserable instead of easy, and the rainy season is a faint memory or future hope, nothing more than a mirage.

Where wells can't be dug, due to lack of underground water sources or some geological reason, a cistern can retain up to 20 percent of water runoff. In the area of Dothan, with up to twenty-eight inches of rainfall a year, a cistern could water five thousand sheep for a year.[1] That's significant for all those dry seasons, for the sheep, for their shepherds, for their owners, and for the economy, because trade depends on product to trade. Without water, everything dies. Eventually.

Jerusalem has so many cisterns underground that it could withstand sieges for long periods. A cistern discovered under the temple mount was forty-three feet deep and could hold two million gallons of water![2] Talk about prepared, in season and out of season.

I wish we could prepare spiritually for dry seasons, could fill ourselves so full that we could live off the reservoir until the next decent rain. I'm not sure that's possible, but surely we can learn how to keep refilling so we never run dry.

This week I realized that my bucket rested on the rocky floor of an empty cistern. For weeks I've rushed through my Scripture reading or cut it short on my way to the next breathless commitment. Silence, praise, and journaling all seemed like tools from a lifetime ago. We moved six weeks ago to a home with great character and vistas. I used to meet the sunrise every morning, spellbound, as it crested the horizon, my soul shouting, "Glory! Glory!" and my soul cistern refilling in a wave.

So as my metal bucket clangs against the limestone lining of my soul, I am forced to rethink refilling. What will it look like in this season? Wishing for last year's rain doesn't help this year's drought. Waiting for the harvest rain doesn't water my soul in its current emptiness.

I decided that I have to keep pumping Scripture into my cistern. Today I went backward in the lectionary to catch yesterday's reading and felt God's grip on my heart like a massage. The lectionary doesn't know that I am spending months and months in Genesis, doesn't know that right now, this very season, Joseph's life and journey have become so important and dear to me.

But there it was, in the lectionary selections: Genesis 37:1–4, 12–28; and Psalm 105. "Here," God whispered to me, "take this cup. Now, drink. See if I don't provide water for you in your wilderness. See if you don't experience my presence, right here, right now, by my leading you to the very passages you are writing about." God all but put the cup at my lips, so clear was this guidance.

This silences my wailing little soul as my impoverished spirit grabs the offering with both hands like a dehydrated baby, *glug-glug-glugging* down the life-giving water. All day today, I taste the water from this morning's reading, savoring God's kindness. And tomorrow?

Fill 'er up again.

TRAVELING MERCY
Dear one,
Water.
Simple
Water.
Not hard.
Find me.
Find water.
There's always water
Somewhere
In the wilderness.

NOTE TO SELF
Fill up the tank today. Tomorrow: repeat.

NOTES
1. John H. Walton, *Genesis* (Grand Rapids: Zondervan, 2013), 123.

2. Bible History, "Ancient Cisterns," accessed December 30, 2014, http://www.bible-history.com/biblestudy/cisterns.html.

ROAD TO FREEDOM

His brothers pulled Joseph up out of the cistern and
sold him for twenty shekels of silver to the
Ishmaelites, who took him to Egypt.

—GENESIS 37:28

Joseph's voice echoed from the bottom of the cavern. It
circled his ears and rang about his head. He crawled to his feet
and craned his neck to see sky above. He heard his brothers
laughing, muted as in a dream. His anger vied with his hurt.
Why? What would cause them to turn on him like that?
Wasn't he following his father's orders? "Here I am, Father.
I'm ready." Five days to get here to see if they were OK.
Well, they weren't OK. They were far from OK. Their minds
unhinged from reason.

Thanks be to God the cistern was dry. Shepherds never
thanked God for an empty cistern, but this shepherd did. His
brothers' voices sounded like they were blowing away in the wind
that swept the grasses. Were they leaving him here in this cave?

His heart pounded. What if Reuben hadn't stepped in?
Joseph would have been dead. How would they have killed
him? A knife? Stoning? Beating him to death? He shuddered,
the damp coolness below ground and the fear shooting shivers
through his aching body.

How long would they leave him here? Wouldn't his father be furious! Then he stopped, mid-thought. What if his brothers rolled the stone over the top? He would die here. No one would ever find him in this cistern.

He flexed his shoulders and moved his limbs. No broken bones after that fall? He gauged the distance to the top. Ten feet? Twenty? Deep enough to be dark, with a peephole of sky above. And no ropes from a lost bucket down here.

The voices doubled in volume. Judah, arguing, pleading for Joseph's life, claiming him as flesh and blood. That was a surprise. New voices joined in. A silhouette of hairy heads peered over the side. Then they all disappeared. Voices haggled in the background, just far enough away that the words ran together like a stream over rocks. A few words emerged. *Strong. Service. Egypt.* Egypt?

Ropes dropped over the side of his tunneled prison. He grabbed on, and his brothers hefted him to the top. He staggered and fell, still shaking, then stood. Merchants with camel-loads of spices waited, beards fluttering in the breeze, even the camels twisting their faces in almost-comic relief. He stared. These men were Ishmaelites. Relatives! Second, third cousins? Sons of his grandpa's half-brother, Ishmael. And Midianites too, perhaps. For a moment he relaxed.

Then the silver changed hands. Joseph counted with the others as the coins clanked into the trader's grimy palm. Twenty! Twenty shekels of silver—two years' worth of wages. His brothers hit pay dirt. Sold! To the men with the bushes on their faces and the camels pawing the loose dirt for effect.

They tied him to the camel with a rope and clamped his neck and ankles with metal. One last look behind him, and there were his brothers. Shouting at him! "Bow down, Joseph, you dreamer! Keep dreaming." Then they divided the silver between them. Their laughter trailed him like a nightmare.

Joseph faced toward Egypt, raising his chin and straightening his shoulders. Though cut to the core by the shackles and his brothers' treason, he would choose, today, to be enslaved to no one by unforgiveness or anger. Today would be the day that began to shape him.

TRAVELING MERCY
Dear one,
Today, you choose.
Who enslaves you,
Holding you captive
Because you carry anger
Or unforgiveness
Toward them?
You may wear metal shackles,
But you needn't be shackled
Any longer
To those who hurt you
Or to those you've hurt.
Today is a new day
To walk forward
Free on the inside.
Without that internal freedom,
Dreams are a mirage.

NOTE TO SELF
Who do I need to forgive? This is No-Shackles Day.

DIRTY DEED

> They got Joseph's robe, slaughtered a goat and
> dipped the robe in the blood.
>
> —Genesis 37:31

Reuben returned after the camel caravan disappeared from sight with Joseph and those traveling salesmen. In despair he tore his clothes in grief, then hurried to his brothers. "The boy isn't there! Where can I turn now?" Then in spite of his good intentions in trying to save Joseph, he joined his brothers in the dirty deed's cover-up.

They slaughtered a goat and doused Joseph's much-envied coat with the animal's blood. Then, the coat weighing heavily on them, they headed back home to their father. If these men had half a conscience and a third of a heart, they would have dreaded the encounter with Jacob. For the five-day journey, the sheep bleating and stalling behind them, they perfected their story.

They offered the robe to Jacob. "We found this. Examine it to see whether it is your son's" (Gen. 37:32). As though there were any doubt given the peculiarities of the coat. They kept up their façade of doubt mingled with curiosity and laced with just a touch of grief and fear. Perfect. Stage-worthy.

Jacob, trembling, reached for the robe. Of course he knew immediately. "It is my son's robe! Some ferocious animal has devoured him. Joseph has surely been torn to pieces" (Gen. 37:33). He imagined his son's pain and fear before the animal killed him. Heartbroken, he tore his clothes in the traditional sign of mourning and grieved for Joseph many days. Far longer than the brothers anticipated. Perhaps in their self-centered dislike for Joseph, they had so hardened their hearts against love and its companion, pain, that they underestimated Jacob's desolation.

All the sons and daughters gathered about him to comfort him, "but he refused to be comforted." "No," he told them all, with their hankies and clucking, "I will continue to mourn until I join my son in the grave" (37:35).

People underestimate mourning, imagining grief fading, turning into a nostalgic, sepia-toned memory and then, finally the picture disappears. No one I know whose child died ever reports a disappearance of grief. At times grief hits them, even years later, a punch in the gut that steals their breath and their composure. At other times, they shake fists into the air, demanding God answer to them for stealing their child. The empty pew at church, the yearly Mother's Day and Father's Day celebrations with all the cookouts, ads, families tromping intact to a restaurant—can there be more painful days?

And grief, with its own timetable for healing, demands restitution for losses. Death of a loved one, of course. But what about death of a relationship, say, by divorce or separation or a move or a misunderstanding or betrayal? Loss of hope or health? Loss of safety in this world? Loss of a dream? So much to grieve, and so little permission for grief in our culture.

Jacob had it right and spoke honestly about losing Joseph. "I will continue to mourn until I join my son in the grave."

Unreleased, grief forms prison bars across our hearts and souls. Finding places for mourning, with people who will sit among the ashes with us, helps us grieve well. Find a place for tears, and find your way, anger and all, to God. God, after all, heals the brokenhearted. And sets the prisoner free.

TRAVELING MERCY
Dear one,
Tears are good.
Tears are holy.
I created them
To help you feel,
To help you heal.
Don't be afraid of the grief.
But don't turn away from me
In your pain,
Because I love you
And long to comfort you
In your suffering.
Take time with your tears.
Take time with me.
Express your anger
And your pain,
And together we will journey
Toward free.
Free to be,
Free to love,
Free to dream.

NOTE TO SELF
Honor grief. It leads to healing.

A DREAM AGENDA

Meanwhile, the Midianites sold Joseph in Egypt to
Potiphar, one of Pharaoh's officials, the captain of the guard.

—Genesis 37:36

Meanwhile. There is always something happening elsewhere,
even in the middle of our greatest anguish. Grief so tightly
clamps around us that it limits our world to our pain. Meanwhile,
as Jacob tore his clothes and wore sackcloth. . . . Thankfully,
this *meanwhile* is a good one, though it would take twenty
years for Jacob to realize it.

While the brothers headed south toward the Valley of Hebron,
the Ishmaelite caravan dragged stumbling Joseph along the
trade route to Egypt. Talk about the journey of a lifetime.
There in that caravan, every inch of the spoiled child Joseph
began to disappear, step by painful step. Sometimes, or often,
the journey toward dream fulfillment looks more like a journey
to humiliation. Or to humility. Or both.

There, on what would become a lifelong sojourn in Egypt,
Joseph began to learn the humility and humiliation necessary
to become a great leader.

But must the school of hard knocks start with Ishmaelites?
Abraham's kin weren't supposed to serve Ishmaelites! They

were the *other* family line. Joseph sure could have gotten his knickers in a knot over that indignity. But cuffed to the caravan, humility lesson number one ensued.

Had Joseph attempted to force his dream to become reality on his own terms, with his shallowness and lack of life experience and wisdom, his family would have been destroyed (or they would have destroyed him, as they attempted to do anyway). As a seventeen-year-old, Papa's favorite son, wearing his special coat, and handsome as all get-out, Joseph was a prime contender to become someone who forced his way through life with a sense of entitlement. People who get everything they want make dangerous dreamers and leaders.

But in God's wisdom, Joseph landed in a cistern, then in a caravan, and then in the service of Potiphar, captain of Pharaoh's guards.

The next leg of learning was just getting started as Joseph exchanged masters from the Ishmaelites to one of Pharaoh's powerful officials. One day he woke up and spouted dreams to his family about his own leadership. And then, just days later, he woke up as a slave. Absolutely no way Joseph envisioned this as the vital course of action to becoming the man in those dreams.

But the details could not have been more perfectly timed. Had Israel sent Joseph to look in on his brothers in virtually any other season, they would have been grazing the flock in the lush grasses of the Valley of Hebron. Had the brothers not headed even farther north to the impressive area of Dothan, a major crossroad for caravans and traders, the details would not have synced with the Ishmaelites' timeline.

Every incident in our lives prepares us for the future God has for us. Every incident. We just need to pay attention in class and do the homework.

TRAVELING MERCY
Dear one,
Not what you expected,
Is it?
This path you tread,
These cuffs about your ankles,
All the *meanwhiles* in your life.
But I'm a really good teacher
In this school of hard knocks,
And my timing couldn't be better
For the details in your life.
So process backward
But face forward,
And remember
That meanwhile
I have a dream
For you.

NOTE TO SELF
Today prepares me for tomorrow. Period.

THE CROOKED (FAMILY) TREE

"I am pregnant by the man who owns these."

—Genesis 38:25

Judah returned with the brothers to break the heartbreaking news of Joseph's supposed death to their father. But Judah didn't stay long in the Valley of Hebron with his testosterone-laden family and the grieving Jacob.

Maybe guilt drove him downhill to Adullam. (Adullam is northwest of Hebron, but at a lower elevation, thus, Judah "went down.") There, Judah married an unnamed Canaanite woman. She conceived quickly and bore three sons. Firstborn Er grew up and married a girl named Tamar, also likely a Canaanite, but he died because he was wicked. According to the culture (and what would become Torah law), the next son, Onan, had to marry his sister-in-law, producing a son for the dead brother.

Onan, knowing the child would legally belong to Er, took measures to ensure that this would not happen (Gen. 38:9). Since this wicked act destroyed the family line, God put Onan to death.

Two down, one to go. Judah supposedly put the third boy, Shelah, too young to marry, on Tamar's dance card for when he grew up. But Judah recognized a pattern (his sons kept dying when they married this woman!), and sent Tamar to live with her father.

Years passed. Judah's wife died and he mourned. And Tamar, of course, noticed that now-grown Shelah wasn't marrying her.

Someone, spying Judah heading to Timnah for sheep-shearing, reported it to Tamar. She changed from her widow's clothing and disguised herself with a veil. She planted herself on Judah's route.

Sure enough, her father-in-law sauntered past, free from mourning and ready for the shearing festivities and accompanying payday. He mistook Tamar for a prostitute, saying, "Come now, let me sleep with you" (Gen. 38:16).

Tamar, nobody's fool, eyed Judah through her veil. "What will you give me to sleep with you?"

How about Judah ships her a goat?

She asked for a pledge, until the goat arrived: Judah's seal, cord, and staff. The seal, in particular, typically unique to its owner, served as a means of identification.

Judah agreed. Once home, his friend attempted to deliver said goat, but returned with goat in tow, not having found the supposed prostitute. Three months passed. Then the town crier told Judah, "Your daughter-in-law Tamar is guilty of prostitution, and as a result she is now pregnant." Judah ordered her burned, a rare punishment reserved for severe sexual crimes.

Though she'd deceived Judah into making love, note how respectfully she presented evidence to the official escorting her to her own execution: "I am pregnant by the man who owns these.... See if you recognize whose seal and cord and staff these are" (Gen. 38:25).

Judah's conscience, God be praised, activated. "She is more righteous than I, since I would not give her to my son Shelah" (38:26). He released her, and one of Tamar's twins, Perez, became the great-great-grandfather of Jesus.

The family line, leading up to the birth of the Messiah, depended on Judah and all the imperfect people on that family tree.

Through Perez, whose name means "break out," God broke through the sin and continued bringing hope. In spite of us, God still accomplishes kingdom purposes through us. God be praised. God will work through the imperfect situations in our lives. And not through a goat, but through a Lamb.

TRAVELING MERCY

Dear one,
Imperfect situation?
Perfect.
Imperfect person?
Perfect.
I will accomplish my perfect will
Through every bit of imperfect in you,
And through,
Or in spite of,
People who are supposed to love you.
Be a real break-out person.
Break out of the mold
And take hold of life—
My life,
My Son's life,
Your life,
Today.

NOTE TO SELF

A break-out person takes hold of life.

A DREAM OF AN INVITATION

"She is more righteous than I."

—GENESIS 38:26

What blushing bride marries expecting husband one and two to both die and leave her childless? Tamar's life was no woman's dream, although if those husbands were that wicked maybe she was better off with them dead. After they died, Judah's family was expected to care for their son's widow. So when Judah shuttled her off to her father's home to presumably await boy-child three's maturity, maybe she figured she'd been shelved. Especially when, years later, boy-child three did not become man-husband three.

Why didn't she remarry? Culture didn't forbid her remarriage. She didn't need to be imprisoned in her widow-wear wardrobe for the rest of her life.

Where on earth did she get the courage to trade out her black mourning clothes for a veil and normal clothing then sit on the roadside waiting for Judah? Though she deceived him into making love with her, we have to admire her tenacity. He had, after all, promised her a husband from the family line.

And why did she want to be part of Judah's family so badly that she would wait . . . and wait . . . and wait?

Is it possible there is one answer to all three questions? Could Tamar's persistence in wanting into the family of Israel have been because of something so appealing she couldn't resist? Some indefinable quality that held her attention relentlessly? She would know of the promise made to Abraham and sons, and the family bore all the evidence of God's blessings. Without knowing the good that would come, she insisted on her rights to be part of Judah's family line. She risked her life to fulfill that desire.

In spite of Judah's inattention to his own promise and duty, he ultimately lived into his name and lived up to his responsibility. He initially told his friend to forget about delivering the goat, lest they become a laughingstock (see Gen. 38:23). But later, he confessed his own unrighteousness by declaring that this woman, who played the harlot in order to continue *his* family line, was more righteous than he. This example of repentance is both captivating and rare.

We know now, of course, that God was behind Tamar's persistence, that this family line would produce the promised Messiah. But skip forward to our lives today. Wouldn't it be remarkable if we lived such lives that people wanted into the family of Abraham's descendant, Jesus the Christ? People aren't exactly clamoring at the church doors to be let in. In fact, one of the common reasons people either leave the church or won't enter in the first place is because of our hypocrisy as individuals and as a corporate entity.

Christians hold no corner on the market of morality. We have, in far too many instances, become the laughingstock that Judah feared. You probably know people who wouldn't stand on the sidewalk outside the church and don't even profess to believe in God let alone follow Christ, but who live honorably and generously and kindly in this world. People who act more like Jesus than you or I do sometimes if we're honest enough to admit it.

How disarming, this confession of Judah's. It figuratively takes away people's weapons when we confess our own hypocrisy and failure to live as we ought. When we don't act as we should and we do act as we shouldn't. Both passive and active sin—we have the market covered on those. But what if we ask for forgiveness from others, because we live in ways that dishonor our family name, the name of Jesus? I don't want to make Jesus look bad any longer.

Though sinful characters fill the storyline, Tamar's story is a call to holiness in the family of God. Your holiness. My holiness. May we become a people who live such bright lives that we issue shining invitations to others to enter, not into a building, but into a forgiveness and freedom found only in Tamar's heir: Jesus, from the tribe of Judah.

Forgiveness. Freedom. Love. A real dream come true.

TRAVELING MERCY

Dear one,
Disarm your weapons
Of defensiveness
And blame.
Ask for forgiveness
As soon as you realize
You've ruptured yet another
Relationship
With me,
With others.
Then see what happens
In the family tree.
It will grow
And produce more fruit
Than you can imagine.
I love you,
I forgive you,
I free you.
Now
Go and do likewise.

NOTE TO SELF

I am the invitation to a heavenly dream.

DREAM POTENTIAL

Potiphar . . . the captain of the guard, bought
[Joseph] from the Ishmaelites.

—GENESIS 39:1

Maybe no one who knew Joseph back then would slate
him for greatness. Maybe no one would scrawl in his yearbook,
"Most likely to succeed." Maybe only similarly spoiled or
snobby teenagers would even like him.

Children are notorious for not accepting others' differences.
Anyone who slips below the norm of average draws fire,
although those with prowess in sports are often welcomed with
open arms. Even being exceptionally smart garners respect in
limited ways. I wonder what happened to the bullied children
on my grade-school playground, what gifts appeared for them,
how they overcame the labels and wounds of childhood. Or *if*
they outgrew them. *If* they discovered gifts and passions and
dreams at all.

Perhaps, if we knew how important Joseph would become,
we'd treat him better. Perhaps, if we recognized in him at
seventeen that in a handful of years he'd be a world leader,
responsible for saving nations of people from famine, we'd
bow down immediately and serve him, coddling him until he

became insufferable. We'd scrape and simper and grovel and spoil.

That would do Joseph absolutely no good in terms of him acquiring wisdom and life experiences that would shape him for leadership.

But what about respecting another's innate gifts, even if those gifts are latent at the moment? Would it change the way we handle others, the way we greet people on the subway or bus, in the hallways or restaurants of our lives? What if we treat everyone as though they have the potential of Joseph? Or the possibilities of, say, Stanley and Livingstone or Stan Mikita or Stan Lee for that matter? What if, every time we meet someone new, we recognize them as human beings, gifted and called, people who just might discover the cure for Alzheimer's disease or radically alter the education and economics of countries ravaged by destitution? Or who will love quietly throughout life? Or simply as someone who deserves love and respect because God says so?

Are we not all Joseph, all possessing the potential to save humanity? And what does salvation look like day after day? Doesn't it look like recognizing another person as someone? As a real live human being who aches and grieves and laughs and dreams. Someone who deserves love, who needs to see love in us in order to understand love from God.

To honor other people in this way is to honor the Joseph in them, to invite them to begin to live into their dreams. How we treat others always reflects how we feel about ourselves, but also reflects our belief in God. The God who crafted the earth with words and separated day from night and water from sky also created us. You, me, the person on the street—all in God's image.

The responsibility is enormous as we move through our days. To recognize another as the image of God, a likeness (sometimes not a very good one) or dim reflection of God.

The slave traders bought Joseph for twenty shekels but saved his life. In turn, a handful of years later, those slave traders would be ravaged by hunger, their lands devastated by famine. Where would they turn for food? To Egypt. To a powerful ruler, more powerful than anyone in the land save Pharaoh. They would turn to Joseph.

Handle with care. Enslave no one with your poor evaluation, your belittling, and your demands.

And let no one enslave you.

TRAVELING MERCY
Dear one,
Your pain and your past
Needn't imprison you,
But rather shapes you
Into your full possibilities.
I see your potential.
I see your pain.
I see the intricate weavings of both.
Live into my love and respect,
And then pass them on
To everyone you meet.
See if you recognize
Me in them.

NOTE TO SELF
Pain, past, possibilities: for me, for others.

THE MAKINGS OF PROSPERITY

The LORD was with Joseph so that he prospered.

—GENESIS 39:2

Just when we think all is lost—Joseph a slave in Egypt! This should not be, not part of the plan. Just when we think, "This situation is irredeemable. No good will come from this." Just when we are ready to throw in the towel and climb out of the ring, we have to keep reading. We can't quit now, not in our own lives or on God. God is going to work it out; there's no way around this truth. God is still God.

So in the darkest cistern of your life, hold tight to that truth, to the God of truth. God will work it out. In the shackles of your journey, though your neck aches from your metal necklace, look beyond the current data. God will work it out. When you land in a veritable widow's prison like Tamar, with a trail of broken promises behind you, hold tight. God will work it out.

Our lives may not look like any of these scenarios, and God's working it out might not look like we hoped—not yet, anyway—but hold on for the long view. God sees the long view and the short view, too. We can't quit, not yet, not until our eyes close for the last time on earth and we wake up in glory. Not till we see the great cloud of witnesses surrounding us and pressing us to the throne of God. And then, quitting won't be part of our heavenly vocabulary.

Unless it's a quitting of regret, of shame over our past, of doubt over God's presence or guidance in our lives. Unless it's a quitting of our shortsighted ways. These, we quit finally in heaven.

But I'm hoping to quit some of this long before landing on heaven's shores. To live shackled to my doubts and misgivings, my guilt and shame, all the ropes of unforgiveness imprisoning me—this is not living. Judah recognized his own sin and got back on track, releasing Tamar from her sin and setting back in motion the wheels of the kingdom.

We don't expect the cisterns and the shackles. We don't expect the abandonment of widowhood. We don't expect slavery of any sort (more about that later). Not only that, but we do not *want* any of this. Most of us aren't masochists who love hardship.

But since when does God meet our expectations? Shouldn't it be the other way around? Shouldn't we be people who seek God and seek to meet his expectations for us? That we walk with integrity, that we love one another, that we view darkness as temporary? For it is, after all, absolutely true.

And since when do we get to decide how God will and will not work and the situations God will and will not allow in our lives? When I look back over my own life, the events I would have loved to slam a six-foot door on and lock out with a hardware store's worth of deadbolts turn out to be times when major character and life development hinged on those very difficulties, those heartbreaks, those door-slamming problems. Had I the choice to stop them—and I'm so grateful that I do not and did not—my life and others' lives would be all the more impoverished.

We do not get to decide or define what prosperity looks like in our lives. The Scriptures tell us, "The LORD was with Joseph so that he prospered." Define *prosper*. Define the Lord being "with us." We can't, because the words are shaped by God around each of us individually. God knew what was coming for Joseph and what he would need to be to accomplish monumental purposes in this world.

Does God not know what is coming for us? Does God not know what it will take, how the word *prosper* will reveal itself in our lives? Of course God knows.

So we do not give up hope, however difficult our shackles. Hope does not disappoint. "We boast in the hope of the glory of God. Not only so, but we also glory in our sufferings, because we know that suffering produces perseverance; perseverance, character; and character, hope. And hope does not put us to shame, because God's love has been poured out into our hearts through the Holy Spirit, who has been given to us" (Rom. 5:2–5).

Sure seems like prosperity to me.

TRAVELING MERCY

Dear one,
I will work it out.
These shackles are not forever.
But my goodness toward you is.
I know what is coming.
I know what it will take
For you to thrive there.
So hold on to hope.
It does not disappoint.
When you trust in me,
I will fill you so full of my love
You will spill over.
Poured in
To pour out.

NOTE TO SELF

Prosperity equals full of God.

OCTOBER DEVOTIONS

TAKE IT TO THE BANK

The LORD was with Joseph so that he prospered, and he
lived in the house of his Egyptian master.

—GENESIS 39:2

The Ishmaelites followed the trade route southward, directly to Pharaoh. They sought out the captain of the guard Potiphar, who knew a good deal when he saw one. One glimpse of strong and good-looking Joseph, and the captain snatched him up for his own household. At that time, Egypt had no actual monetary currency; people were paid either by bartering or with land or farming privileges. Whatever he traded to the Ishmaelites in order to own Joseph, Potiphar made the wisest purchase of his lifetime.

God blessed the house of Potiphar with Joseph in residence. And Potiphar recognized God's blessing. We heave a sigh of relief. Not everyone gives credit where credit is due. Plenty of people take any prosperity as their due and forget to notice or honor the people who helped.

But Potiphar connected the dots: Joseph . . . prosperity . . . God. God led Joseph to him. God gave Joseph wisdom, and Joseph put it to use in Potiphar's service. "Joseph found favor in his eyes and became his attendant" (Gen. 39:4). The

Scriptures detail prosperity upon prosperity and the increasing responsibility Joseph assumed.

To strive for another's wellbeing, for someone else's prosperity, this is the mark of the ideal employee and a future leader, someone able to see the big picture in spite of personal involvement in small details. Joseph expected nothing but gave everything. It takes a servant heart and real love to work for the benefit of others, knowing that you might never get a raise, award, or gold watch at retirement.

But what is interesting is the Scriptures say that "the LORD was with Joseph so that *he* prospered" (emphasis added). Joseph prospered in that servant state, in that place of submission. He grew in favor with the captain of the guard. He continued to rise through the ranks of the captain's household until his master trusted him even with the bookkeeping, the accounting, the very inner workings of the home and the business profit and loss sheets. According to job descriptions in ancient documents, the role of steward also included overseeing the fields and farming of their masters. So Joseph even oversaw the work of the fields. God prospered Joseph in that way too.

This isn't always the case for all the people like you and me. We sometimes don't get the raise or the new title. Sometimes we toil away in obscurity, doing our best for the boss but never receiving any sort of earthly reward or recognition.

We take heart because surely Joseph also prospered and grew in character, his past and the privileges of his past growing ever more distant until they disappeared on the horizon called long ago. His favor with the captain would have ceased had

Joseph retained any trace of the tattling son, his papa's pet, the one with the beautiful, distinct, and ultimately dangerous coat.

Joseph lost his coat of distinction, but he gained the cloak of God's favor. Joseph prospered because God was with him. And when God designs our cloak of prosperity, I hope we have the eyes to recognize it.

TRAVELING MERCY

Dear one,
Take heart.
I will see that you prosper
In a way that I recognize
In heaven,
Whether or not others honor you
Or even notice.
Joseph prospered
In the ways best for him.
And so will I prosper you
In the ways best for you
And your future
And all that we get to do
Together.
I will design your cloak
Personally.

NOTE TO SELF

Wear God's cloak. Not someone else's.

APPROVED

Joseph found favor in his eyes and became his attendant.

—GENESIS 39:4

It's brilliant and nearly unbelievable. All trace of Jacob's spoiled and favored son disappeared in Joseph's journey from slave to servant, to attendant, to household manager, and to supervisor of all that Potiphar owned. Joseph's silver spoon disappeared somewhere between the cistern and slave route and Egypt, and a work ethic of integrity and honor prevailed in its place. Because of Joseph, his master saw the bloom of fortune in all that he owned, in house and in field. Joseph rose to such a position in that household that there was no one more important.

Joseph was undoubtedly a quick study. He applied himself to all his labor, and bettered himself en route. To reach that level of authority meant he had to be literate and smart. His Hebrew lessons wouldn't help him much when learning to read and write the difficult Egyptian language. Joseph likely worked more than forty hours a week without two days off and time to go to church. So he toiled overtime to improve himself. He took notes, he probably went without sleep to study at night, and he did whatever it took to serve well in a position he never imagined for himself. His teachable spirit is a key mark of a leader and of a person who lives into dreams.

This exhausts me. In a world where media-craziness runs rampant, in an industry where success supposedly hinges on how many hours are put into social media venues, how many people read our blog or "like" us, and whether we appear on page one of an Internet search—I'm wasted just thinking about it.

But maybe our growth curve is arched specifically for each of us. My growth curve might look like trusting God more and getting a little more sleep. It might look like a longer period of worship and prayer or Scripture memory. Maybe my growth curve involves the discipline of community, deliberately reaching out to colleagues and neighbors and would-be friends. Maybe even people from different roads than the ones I've trod.

A growth curve, coupled with a teachable spirit is what God will tailor for us. Joseph needed to learn everything necessary for his position as a servant. And in our positions as servants, so do we. Where do you need to improve your service? How about asking someone you love, "How could I help you today with everything on your shoulders?"

My friend asked her husband, "What areas would you really like me to grow in? What bothers you about some of my habits?" It took courage, I think, but he searched for a few examples (and to both their credit, came up with only a couple), and she tries to eliminate those from the trail she leaves through each day.

A teachable spirit, the sign of a leader, the sign of someone who lives toward dreams. It sounds a lot like the words Paul wrote to Timothy: "Do your best to present yourself to God as one approved, a worker who does not need to be ashamed and who correctly handles the word of truth" (2 Tim. 2:15).

TRAVELING MERCY

Dear one,
Do your best.
Be diligent
To present yourself
To me,
And let me design your growth curve.
Let's figure out together
How to improve your service
And your teachable spirit,
Not afraid to be wrong,
To learn how to live right,
Uprightly,
All the marks of a leader.
Do your best.
Let me take care of the rest.

NOTE TO SELF

Be teachable.

TRUSTWORTHY

Potiphar put him in charge of his household, and he
entrusted to his care everything he owned.

—Genesis 39:4

Whom do you trust with everything you own? Everything. Every single penny, dollar, investment, possession, and person? Every hope, dream, delight, and doubt? Every process, job, employee, and event? Potiphar trusted Joseph so completely that he worried about absolutely nothing. He didn't worry about his family, staff, bookwork, fields, crops, or home. He worried about exactly one thing: the food he ate.

It's nice work if you can get it.

But seriously, whom do you trust with everything? If we could trust more, we'd probably need a lot less anti-anxiety medication. Unless it's a chronic chemical imbalance, so much of worry, at least so much of my own worry, is related to trust. Or rather, to a lack of trust. I don't trust myself to complete things in a timely fashion (largely because I expect far more than I can pack into waking hours without stealing some from sleep). I rarely trust others with really vital details, at least not without a few hundred texts and notes to remind them of those details.

And don't you have a list a mile long of all the times you've trusted others and they haven't delivered? They haven't delivered in exactly the manner you expected or didn't meet your exacting standards. In some way, large or small, you've been betrayed. And the cumulative effect of betrayal? Distrust.

Maybe our lack of trust isn't limited to human beings or human systems (like government websites or the phone company). Maybe our lack of trust in the big and small things we pin on God. We don't trust God with everything. We don't trust God to cover all the bases. We don't trust God's taste in details. How about God's timing? How about that little detour, that cistern back in the field or that slave trader? God seems to let so many hard things slip by, and sometimes we just don't trust any longer.

It's a little off track to think about all the people we don't trust and all the ways we don't trust God without talking about our own trustworthiness. I know what I'm made of. I stumble, flail, and fall. I forget. I am prone to failure.

So the record in Genesis of Joseph's relationship with Potiphar is all the more remarkable. Consider Joseph's background. Consider all the idiosyncrasies he could have developed. Consider the baggage he could lug around with him. (I'm still ticked at those brothers, however wounded they might have been by their father's treatment of little bro Joe.) Joseph's journey to Potiphar's doorstep was on the brink of disastrous rerouting. And it would get worse before it got better.

But Potiphar trusted Joseph with absolutely everything. Nothing was off-limits according to the Scriptures. We can't read this as "Joseph was perfect," but we can read this as Joseph constantly improved his service. He kept growing, and as he grew, he gained more of Potiphar's trust.

Psalm 37:3 says, "Trust in the LORD, and do good. Dwell in the land and enjoy safe pasture." Joseph trusted in God and did all the good he possibly could. And Potiphar noticed. Potiphar trusted. And when that trust was broken, even then, the master of the house would show favor to Joseph.

To live toward the dream, we increase in our trustworthiness. One little task at a time.

TRAVELING MERCY

Dear one,
Trust when you cannot see the future
Or the reasons for the past
Or the rationale behind today's events.
That trust is possible
Only when you trust
The God you cannot see,
Working through
Events you cannot understand.
I plant dreams in your heart,
And I help fulfill those dreams
One step at a time.
And that's how you trust—
One step,
One minute,
One event,
At a time.
Trust me,
And grow more trustworthy.

NOTE TO SELF

Improve my service.

SWEAT DREAMS
(NO, IT'S NOT A TYPO!)

So Potiphar left everything he had in Joseph's care.

—GENESIS 39:6

Remember when people signed yearbooks in high school? How many times did the salutation read, "To a sweat girl"? "To a real sweat boy"? Sweet though they may be, dreams require a little or a lot of sweat. All dreams, whether we think they come from God or from our gifts and talents (or likely, both) ultimately demand, at some point, human effort. There is nothing magic about dreams, not the dreams Joseph dreamed or the dreams you woke up with last night or last year or last decade. Dreams necessitate our cooperation with the process. God doesn't do a heavenly zapping and doors fling open and opportunity flies through. Not always. Sometimes. (Though usually to others.) But almost always our effort and choice figure into the equation.

Joseph made definite decisions on the way to Egypt. He cooperated with the dream's learning curve. And all dreams have those curves; sometimes they look like hairpin switchbacks on a skinny, narrow road, and sometimes they are lovely hills and dells and gentle bends in the country highway.

God's hand was on Joseph, of course. But Joseph didn't slouch up to the slave market and fight back, screaming insolence or issuing petty statements like, "You don't know who I am. You can't treat me like this. I was stolen. Slavery is illegal." (There is a place for shouting against poor treatment, against being sold into the slave trade, against abuse of any form. There on the block was not that place. Also, slavery was just beginning in Egypt during the Middle Kingdom period, so there were few specific rules anyway.)

Our dreamer, though frightened when sold into slavery, didn't let fear freeze him in his previous entitlement mentality. Had Joseph not squared his shoulders when put on the auction block in Egypt, not assumed an aura of confidence and competence, Potiphar might have moved right past him.

Further, Joseph refused the handicap of anger turned to bitterness. Both fear and bitterness catch us and trip us, if they don't thicken our arteries and veins and give us a heart attack first.

So Joseph, there in Potiphar's household, worked from a divine plan, a plan guaranteed to bring results: Do the work in front of you. Work with excellence. Learn everything possible, even if it's not related to your current job description. Speak the language of the people around you, and if you don't already know it, learn it. No matter how difficult. Whether that language is tech-speak or colloquial, whether it's the language of industry or of servitude, learn the language. The more we know, the more valuable we become to people en route. Potiphar watched Joseph work. He observed his ethics. He increased his slave's responsibility, rewarding the behavior he witnessed.

That Potiphar rewarded Joseph is fabulous. But even more importantly, Potiphar recognized the One who led and inspired Joseph, the One who planted dreams in Joseph, the One whom Joseph was learning to serve. Potiphar identified the source of his own prosperity: God, blessing Joseph, and then as a result blessing him.

We see the outworking of the original promise back in Genesis 12:1–4, that Abraham and his descendants would be a blessing, that God would bless those who bless them.

Joseph was blessed by his hard work, by paying attention to details, by faithfulness to the little things. Paul might have been referring to Joseph's spiritual work ethic when he wrote, "Slaves, in all things obey those who are your masters on earth, not with external service, as those who merely please men, but with sincerity of heart, fearing the Lord. Whatever you do, do your work heartily, as for the Lord rather than for men, knowing that from the Lord you will receive the reward of the inheritance. It is the Lord Christ whom you serve" (Col. 3:22–24 NASB). Joseph did his work heartily, as unto God, not just unto human beings, not just as unto the man who owned him.

It's a win-win-win situation: Joseph wins favor with Potiphar; Potiphar's estate prospers as a result; and God gets the glory on all fronts.

Do the dream. Work the dream. Live the dream.

TRAVELING MERCY

Dear one,
I love, love, love
That you look beyond
Your current situation to me.
That you decide today (and tomorrow)
To trust me
And trust the people en route to the dream,
And to become proficient
In the tasks before you.
Even if they seem menial,
You will learn,
You will grow.
And you already find
Favor with me.
Keep dreaming.
Keep doing.
Keep working.
Keep living.
And keep your eyes
On me.
I have you covered.

NOTE TO SELF

Dream: work it, learn it, live it.

DESTRUCTIVE DISTRACTIONS

After a while his master's wife took notice of Joseph.

—GENESIS 39:7

Turns out that Potiphar should have concerned himself with at least one additional area of life besides his meals: his wife. Bored to distraction by all the catering and riches, she took a fancy to the handsome, well-built Joseph, the one her husband entrusted with absolutely everything.

She fancied that Hebrew, with his broad shoulders and his strange language and his, ah . . . service. She tried repeatedly to get his attention, but his attention to details included everything and everyone except her.

She decided to break through his demeanor with bluntness: "Come to bed with me!"

Unbelievably, at least in her own estimation, he refused her. Refused *her*. "Everything he owns he has entrusted to my care. . . . My master has withheld nothing from me, except you," Joseph said (Gen. 39:8–9). Imagine! Then he prattled on about wickedness, how wicked it would be for him to take her.

Wicked? Her attention shifted from his honor and integrity to how she could grab him. She sharpened her hooks. No one would refuse her without feeling her wrath. So she fixed all her attention on winning this man to her bed. Daily she beguiled him. Daily he spurned her advances.

One day, Joseph clocked in for work at an empty house. No one there. If only he'd turned and run the other way, but searching the palace for others, he found her. Or, rather, she found him. She clutched at him and snagged her claws in his cloak. "Come to bed with me!" She should have been embarrassed at how often he'd refused her, but rejection only strengthened her intent.

She underestimated Joseph and his trustworthiness. He fled from her, pulling from her grasp and running from the house. But she had his coat. (These coats of Joseph kept landing him in trouble, one way or the other.) She let out a wail that would make your hair fall out. Help poured in from the streets. She claimed assault, and then held on to the cloak-and-swagger story until her husband's shadow fell through the door.

With no witnesses, her lie stuck.

To list some obvious truths about self-protection: Don't be alone in a house, car, or office with a person of the opposite sex. Especially with someone who has made repeated advances. Keep a witness, keep a door open to the next person's office, and keep yourself and your reputation safe. And run. Run for your life. (Also, try to bring your cloak with you.)

Not everyone lands on both feet after a debacle of these proportions. Sometimes such setbacks entirely jettison dreams, shooting holes in their fragile wings. Still, we can't stop dreaming, and we can't relax our vigilance.

But remember this: Even when false claims follow you, God is bigger than any falsehood. And seeming detours make the best stories as life and dreams unfold. Because eventually, you will be in the right place at just the right time.

TRAVELING MERCY
Dear one,
I will cloak you
With my compassion
And lead you
To the right junction.
Meanwhile,
Watch your back,
Behave with integrity,
Remember the dream,
And be wise.
Don't let another's folly
Force you into unforgiveness
Or folding in your dream.
We are right on track.

NOTE TO SELF
Take care, beware, and be wise.

BORED HOUSEWIFE SYNDROME

She caught him by his cloak and said, "Come to bed with me!"
—Genesis 39:12

A rich, bored, Nile River reality-show housewife. Potiphar's wife got whatever she wanted, and if she didn't, she stirred up a beehive of trouble for anyone not granting her wishes and whims. Too bad for that person who denied her. Too bad when her screech of accusation landed people in dungeons.

Maybe, though, we can see through her boredom, her riches, her spoiled indolence, and her indulgence. Maybe, if we look closely enough, if we ignore her grasping, painted fingernails and her sharp tongue, her hook-or-crook means of satisfaction—maybe we can see what she really wants.

Boredom combined with wealth creates a deadly synergy, especially when there's no moral grounding and no dream for positive impact and influence in this world. But go deeper and we find a woman who is, quite possibly, just one toy among many. Another beautiful face without what she's really hoping for: a love that lasts forever. An "I do" that also means "I always will."

Consider her husband's reaction: He burned with fury but then threw Joseph into a prison reserved for officials of Pharaoh, for important people. Even more telling, the prison was evidently in Potiphar's own house. Had he seriously considered Joseph a threat, he'd have sent him off to be executed pronto. Further, Genesis 39:19 tells us he burned with fury when his wife accused his most valued servant of rape—but it isn't clear if he's angry with his wife because he is well-acquainted with her ways or if he's angry with Joseph.

Either way, Potiphar's response tells us something about him and about his wife. He apparently doesn't put much stock in her accusation. And he doesn't, evidently, waste much love on her.

Maybe at first it wouldn't have been a waste. Maybe at first he loved and trusted her. Showered her with love and affection. Maybe. But now? Now she'd shown herself, and likely more than once, to be a woman who couldn't be trusted with other men.

But wait. Isn't there a "Potiphar's wife" in all of us, whether we are men or women? Aren't we all prone to wander, prone to leave the God we love? Don't we, just about every other moment, gaze at forbidden fruit and want some for ourselves? Whether the fruit is someone else's spouse or house, someone's cloak or carriage, of course we do. Our nation has been built on the premise that we want what others have and, more than that, in some sense we deserve it and will do just about anything to get it.

Thankfully, our God has a track record of inviting us, always, back into relationship, no matter how we've flung ourselves at other gods and other people. No matter our adultery, our crime, the laziness, the lies, God calls us back and reinstates us. God honors the relationship with us that initiates in heaven. God doesn't turn a blind eye to our wanderings, to our Potiphar's-wife type behaviors. But rather, challenges us to return, to acknowledge our wrong turns and ruptures of relationship, and to be loved.

TRAVELING MERCY
Dear one,
Turn your gaze away from your sin,
Away from your lust.
Direct your focus toward me,
And notice your deepest desire,
Deeper than your wants—
The longing to be fully
And always loved.
My "I do" is never "I don't"
Or "I'm through,"
But always "I do."
Do you?
Then return to me.
I forgive you,
And I do not count
Your sins against you.
Just return.

NOTE TO SELF
Where is my "I do"?

THE BARS OF OPPORTUNITY

Joseph's master took him and put him in prison.

—GENESIS 39:20

Seeing his wife with Joseph's incriminating coat, Potiphar blew a fuse. Aflame with fury, he threw Joseph in prison.

Being on the wrong side of an adultery charge did not bode well for Joseph. Before you say, "Duh, really?" know that most crimes in that time and place typically met with execution, maiming or mutilation, or a fine. But adultery often led straight to execution. In fact, very few records exist of jail in Joseph's day; Egypt was one of the few countries with prisons. Prison is not included in the punishments in the Torah, and no records evidently exist of Hebrew prisons. This adds credence to Joseph's life story.

That Potiphar locked Joseph in prison rather than ordering immediate execution issued a clear statement about Joseph's worth and the weight Potiphar put on his wife's story. And Joseph's cellmates were political prisoners, people who held positions of power in Pharaoh's organization.

From a cistern to a slave caravan, to a servant, to a household manager, the steward of everything Potiphar owned. The perfect trajectory for our dreamer. But now, because of a lust-filled and bored woman, Joseph landed in prison. How demoralizing, just when everything had been going so swimmingly.

Joseph's story is ours as well (hopefully without the reality show auditions, however, and the camera crews): from good to better, to terrible, to wait-it-gets-worse. It's the storyline of great drama and great lives, though it doesn't seem to fit into any dream sequence we might imagine. Except perhaps a nightmare storyboard.

Daily details of Joseph's life didn't make the history books. But the dailyness of God's faithfulness appears again and again. Genesis 39:20–21 states, "But while Joseph was there in the prison, the LORD was with him; he showed him kindness and granted him favor in the eyes of the prison warden."

Just as Joseph proved himself trustworthy to Potiphar, and God blessed him with greater responsibility and greater favor, so Joseph showed himself to be reliable to the warden. In a thankless job (wardens ranked fairly low on popularity polls, just guessing), anyone who doesn't make life harder rises above the crowd. But someone who makes your job and life easier, actively easing the difficulty of the work, becomes a favorite. Yes, the Lord was with Joseph and blessed him and Joseph acted faithfully. And he grew in favor with the warden, rising in the ranks of responsibility, even while in prison.

That might not be your life's path so far. Not only do most of us not act like Joseph, but most of us might not be very good sports in prison on a false charge. But it's not too late, not ever too late, to begin to view the bars of our lives as enclosing a place for God to bless. Life's limitations may be

God's opportunities for growing in humility and in service to others and to God.

Our lives, like Joseph's, may seem less than dreamlike right now. But if this is where we are, then this is where God allowed us to be. Today, I'm looking through the bars of limitation and disappointment, trusting that God will give me the grace to love well here and teach me to serve well here.

TRAVELING MERCY
Dear one,
Growing in humility
Seems like
An oxymoron.
But humility fertilizes
Great dreams.
So serve
And give
And grow
Right here,
Today.
And I'll stand guard.
I never leave my post.

NOTE TO SELF
Limitations are opportunities in disguise.

A DREAM JOB

Pharaoh was angry with his two officials . . .
and put them in custody.

—Genesis 40:2–3

Sometimes, the prisons of the unexpected bring out our gifts. I doubt Joseph counted on that happening, as he rose through the ranks of the prison. His recordkeeping skills and his mastery of the Egyptian language would be handy in prison as he kept track of prisoners and offenses, dates and punishments. Before long, the warden worried about absolutely nothing with Joseph around.

This is starting to sound like a familiar description for Joseph. His character is forming, and now we wonder if when he raced back from the fields to tattle on his brothers' work, if maybe he actually knew what he was talking about. He was in training for excellence. Which is a good motto for dreamers in general, because dreams are innocuous as long as all we do is dream.

Converting dreams to reality, however, requires excellence. Even in a prison cell. And excellence means plain hard work.

The atmosphere in a prison, whether in 1600 BC or today, isn't particularly conducive to excellence. It is, however, excellent for developing bitterness, blame, lethargy, depression, aggression, and lack of cooperation. So for Joseph to so consistently build on his reputation for excellence means he refused to allow his emotions to reign. Negativity destroys dreams or at least delays them.

Pushing toward excellence creates an opening for opportunity, and opportunity landed in Joseph's lap when his new cellmates entered: the chief baker and the chief cupbearer for Pharaoh. Officials entrusted with safety and satisfaction, they'd risen that morning on the wrong side of Pharaoh, who tossed them into prison amid some conspiracy theories.

After some time, these inmates awakened from disturbing dreams. Joseph checked on them and noticed their glumness. "Why do you look so sad today?" (Gen. 40:7). (Another sign of excellence: emotional presence and paying attention to people's demeanor.)

"We both had dreams . . . but there is no one to interpret them" (see 40:1–8). And Joseph, who must have recognized all along that God gave him favor (rather than thinking his own gifts of service and intelligence brought him favor), turned all dreams over to God. "Do not interpretations belong to God? Tell me your dreams" (40:8).

The chief cupbearer spun his tale of a vine, three branches, and the rapid production of blooms turning to grapes, squeezed by his own hand into Pharaoh's cup. Joseph listened, heard the meaning behind it all, and interpreted: three branches equaled three more days in prison, and then the man would be back on the job.

The baker's dream panned out to be less auspicious with three baskets sitting on his head and birds eating breads from those baskets. In three days, he would be decapitated and his body impaled on a pole. *Gulp*.

Joseph's final words to the cupbearer were, "Remember me and show me kindness; mention me to Pharaoh and get me out of this prison" (40:14).

But while the cupbearer forgot, God did not. And meanwhile, the gift for interpreting dreams ignited, there in that prison where an innocent man languished, waiting to be remembered.

TRAVELING MERCY

Dear one,
Watch for new gifts,
For surprising twists
In the plot of your life,
Even though you are not where you wanted to be,
Even though life is not what you expected.
Pay attention to others,
Hear their hopes and dreams,
And live toward excellence.
I will be right on time
With the next installment
Of your story.
I promise.

NOTE TO SELF

Dreams need details. Notice them.

SEEING IN THE DARK

"Remember me and show me kindness."

—GENESIS 40:14

Joseph, certain of God's interpretation of the cupbearer's dream, asked only one thing of his fellow prisoner: "But when all goes well with you, remember me and show me kindness; mention me to Pharaoh and get me out of this prison" (40:14).

In the darkness of prison, in the bleakness of the unexpected, in spite of trying to be faithful and striving to serve and offer excellence, discouragement dogs us all. Joseph begged the cupbearer to remember him and show kindness just as Joseph showed him kindness. He didn't want to stay in prison one minute longer than necessary, however much favor and status he gained there in the eyes of the warden, the inmates, and the prison hierarchy.

It doesn't seem too much to ask. Show a little love to the person who helped you. But the man forgot. When Pharaoh sprung him from prison, the cupbearer helped arrange a big bash for Pharaoh, the baker lost his head, and life went on. The cupbearer got caught up in all the plots and subplots and machinations of the kingdom, and flat out forgot Joseph, the one who comforted him in prison, showed him kindness, and offered him hope.

Genesis 40:23 tells us, "The chief cupbearer, however, did not remember Joseph; he forgot him." Not only did he not remember; he forgot. The double emphasis speaks of heartache and discouragement in that prison.

The Scriptures don't tell us whether Joseph daily remembered his own dreams back in the Valley of Hebron, back in his brash youthfulness and all that bowing down business. Who knows how often Joseph took out the dreams, examined them, spit-polished them, and asked God what they meant, since he seemed to be forgotten in prison? Not exactly a dream-fulfillment center.

This glimpse of the real Joseph—the Joseph hurting in prison, the Joseph who'd been ripped from his family, stripped, stolen, sold, enslaved, and falsely accused—gives hope for all of us who feel broken by our circumstances but want to be faithful. Joseph simply acknowledged the truth: "I was forcibly carried off from the land of the Hebrews, and even here I have done nothing to deserve being put in a dungeon" (40:15).

A little honesty about our situation helps us square up and face forward. We're in a dungeon, a bleak prison. This is terrible. We're sick and tired of making scratches on the wall to count the days. We, unlike Joseph, quite possibly deserve to be here. But that it's lousy, dark, hopeless, and the wait interminable remains without question. There's no shame in admitting this. Painting a glossy picture of our lives in a despairing cell does a disservice to anyone who suffers.

Focusing on the God who breaks down prison doors and sets prisoners free, however, takes us even deeper into honest appraisal of our situation. Honesty helps us see in the dark. It's bad, yes. But God is big. Bigger than our prison. God is not bound by bars on windows or locks on doors. Our Jesus walks through walls. Our Jesus finds us in the dark and says, "I have come to set prisoners free. I have not forgotten you. I always remember you."

So in the dark, in the fear, in the abyss of anonymity, we cling to the God who remembers us and remembers that dream. One day, God will spring us and fling us into the wide-open spaces of freedom. Until then, we cling.

TRAVELING MERCY
Dear one,
You're not forgotten.
So acknowledge the truth:
Life is hard.
But I'm remembering
A child who dreamed big dreams,
So remember me.
Remember those dreams
And trust that the bars
Are not permanent,
But my love is.

NOTE TO SELF
Honesty helps me see in the dark.

NOT AGAIN

"I have done nothing to deserve being put in a dungeon."

—GENESIS 40:15

Just when you think you have it made, someone blows a shrill whistle filled with lies and you find yourself protesting, "Not again. No, please. Not again." Remember when Joseph's brothers pitched him into the dark cistern? The Hebrew word for pit, for cistern (Gen. 37:22, 24) is the same word used for dungeon, where Potiphar threw Joseph after his encounter with Mrs. Potiphar. Cistern, pit, dungeon. There seems to be no end to the possibilities for places of punishment or confinement.

Sometimes, people say to me, "I really want to understand this trial or difficulty. I want to navigate it well. I just want to get it right so I don't have to go through this again." And I want to pat them on the back and say, "Hope that works for you." Not to be sarcastic at all. I hope right along with them that they don't have to go through that pit again.

But to be realistic, we will never be able to avoid pits, cisterns, or figurative prisons. Not this side of the final Promised Land. Every single day, the possibilities are endless for the pits of relationship collapses, dysfunction, disappointment, and other hardship. The type of pit changes, perhaps (although a remarkable number of people keep falling into the same hole, myself included), but the fact of the pit, never. We're like hunters who creep through the jungle. With every step, we face the likelihood of crashing through a veneer of leaves and branches that disguises yet another dungeon or cistern. Another place of squeezing darkness and damp uncertainty. Of fear or pain.

So as we navigate our present jungle, absolutely we ask what God wants us to learn from the current problem. How God wants us to seek heaven from this hole we find ourselves in. How God wants to change us, our heart, our focus, or our direction with each tumble.

But this won't eliminate the next pit or prison. It will, however, give us practice in not succumbing to the discouragement there. It will help us to recognize, "Aha, I've seen your likes before. I have your number, and you're not going to win." It will help us to declare the truth: God is victor over every prison and pit we encounter and invades every cistern and dungeon. Every single one. God is not limited by walls made with human hands or contained by the limestone lining of the next cistern. God permeates all barriers and finds us in the pit.

This pit. And the next one.

The dungeons won't last forever because one day the warden will come in a hurry with jangling keys and unlock our door and push us toward the showers. We will receive clean, new clothes and rush into never-ending daylight, toward the dream we've all been waiting for, the dream with outlines we've scratched into all the walls that squeeze around us, the hieroglyphics of hope.

Heaven. It's called heaven.

TRAVELING MERCY

Dear one,
The cisterns aren't part of your dream,
But you can't sidestep those pits.
Still you might miss my plan
For you in the pits,
So hold out your hand
And look to me.
Decide to learn from this pit.
It will prepare you for the next.
And processing every single pitfall
Prepares you for heaven.
Scratch those hieroglyphics of hope
On the wall of your soul,
Because I'm coming for you.

NOTE TO SELF

The pit is a place of possibility.

LONG NIGHT WATCHES

On my bed I remember you; I think of you through the
watches of the night. Because you are my help, I sing in the shadow
of your wings. I cling to you; your right hand upholds me.

—PSALM 63:6–8

Inside that dungeon, light rarely penetrated, if ever. No
corner cells with prime location-location-location advantages.
The ringtone of Joseph's desperate plea to the cupbearer
echoes throughout centuries in the penal system. As does one
antidote to discouragement: the power of music.

King David said many years later from a place of despair
and longing, "I sing in the shadow of your wings" (Ps. 63:7).
To ward off the internal night, the eternal feeling of darkness,
he sang. What about Paul and Silas, locked in prison, praying
and singing hymns to God? The other prisoners listened
along, when "suddenly there was such a violent earthquake
that the foundations of the prison were shaken. At once all
the prison doors flew open, and everyone's chains came
loose" (Acts 16:26).

Those descriptors equal power: suddenly, violent, earthquake,
foundations shaken, doors flying open, chains loose. Why?

Paul and Silas were singing. Squished in their cell, chained
there in the dark, singing. And everyone nearby listened to them

singing. Paul and Silas were perhaps not first-century Luciano Pavarottis or Josh Grobans. And probably people listened, not because they were bored with nothing else to do (although that is likely true), but because the music offered them hope. Singing opens our hearts to longing and reminds us of a truth deeper than our current circumstances. Not only does singing remove us temporarily from despair, but worship music focuses us on God. It trains our hearts and our minds.

Stories from concentration camps during World War II detail the power of music. Prisoners sang classics, ditties, hymns, and Scriptures. They sang, and music pushed away the demon of depression and fed their souls. Imagine the impoverished conditions, the torture and horror. And then the prisoners, determined to fight back with the music in their memories.

The enemy will never win with music as our weapon of choice. Whether it's "Jesus Loves Me" or a lullaby, whether it's Scripture sung to music or hymns repeated throughout the ages, sing. Whether belting current praise music or humming tunelessly under your breath, sing. Worship is one of the most oft-repeated commandments in the Bible. Whether or not you feel like singing, sing.

Music converts our prison into a heavenly portal. So we, with David, sing through the watches of the night, and music helps us cling to the God of all the earth and the God of our tiny prison cells. Under the shelter of God's wings, we sing, and music wings our hearts free of jail and off to heavenly places. It restores our souls, reminds us of God's power and presence, and leads us back toward hope.

TRAVELING MERCY

Dear one,
Joyful noise
Makes me smile,
And directing music toward me
Changes you,
Changes directions,
Keeping your heart alive and pliable.
Worship leads you out of the darkness
Into the light.
Your praise
Is music to my ears.
So sing,
And see if you notice
Me singing along
With you.

NOTE TO SELF

Cling and sing.

MEAN BO⅃S

Grow a wise heart—you'll do yourself a favor;
keep a clear head—you'll find a good life.

—PROVERBS 19:8 MSG

Mean people exist. Get over it. Get on with your dream. Learn what you can from the meanies and don't become one yourself. Understand that people are mean because they are jealous, insecure, wounded, or just plain lost and far from God. Maybe they've never been loved. It's no excuse for meanness, but it makes psychological and emotional sense, which helps us understand others' packaging or context.

Mean people don't have to become your special project, necessarily—constantly helping someone who abuses you emotionally probably helps neither of you. Mean people need emotional healing that no one else can do for them. Joseph's brothers, meanies that they were, jealous and jumpy with itchy trigger fingers, needed to encounter grief (their father's), guilt (their own), and hunger (everyone's, though when it became personal, then they really would learn). They needed to face the effects of their own meanness and grow up. Chronological age—all but one was older than seventeen-year-old Joseph—is no predictor of emotional maturity.

Meanness, once we're aware of it, becomes a choice. Though he chose mockery and belittling alongside his brothers on that fateful day outside Dothan, Judah exhibited a conscience when he convinced his brothers not to kill Joseph, but rather to sell him to the Ishmaelites. Later, it appears that Judah learned humility in his interaction with Tamar, when he admitted, "She is more righteous than I" (Gen. 38:26).

Life comes with a learning curve. We learn through what we see and experience, and though our natures are bent toward evil, God invites us into salvation and into upward emotional and spiritual movement. Once we accept that in ourselves and others, we begin to be free to grow ourselves. Another's assessment of us or their meanness to us no longer controls or hinders us, but rather becomes a stepstool to help us reach higher.

We choose to reach, to grow. We choose to listen to the dreams planted within us and give no one else the power to shoot holes in the dream or in us. Hopefully, rather than leaning toward mean ourselves, we become the example for others to follow—people who choose to ride the learning curve upward rather than blame the mean people, the people who wounded us. Holding on with both hands, white-knuckling it, and pressing our feet into the floorboards maybe, but upward.

Like others, we choose, too. Others choose mean; we choose dreams.

TRAVELING MERCY
Dear one,
Don't shoot holes
In your own dreams.
Don't lean toward mean.
But choose to live higher.
Choose to live freer.
Choose to live wiser.
Ride the rails of growth upward,
And enjoy the view.

NOTE TO SELF

Dream cancels mean.

PREREQUISITE TO DREAM-COME-TRUE TIME

In Christ God was reconciling the world to himself,
not counting people's trespasses against them, and he
has given us the message of reconciliation.

—2 CORINTHIANS 5:19 NET

To meet Cynthia (not her real name), you would never suspect the deep chasms pain once carved within her, never know the terror of her childhood. She is vivacious, brilliant, loving, warm, compassionate, and deep. Her faith flows through her pores and pours from her in words and deeds. Her exuberance and energy never dribble away, at least, they never have in the years of our friendship.

Raised in an alcoholic and abusive family, Cynthia never knew safety. Then friends invited her into their family life and, as a young teenager, her hunger for stability and hope met the love of God. She came to know Jesus and his amazing gift of life and forgiveness, and with that, his freedom. She gobbled up truth and kindness, ingesting every morsel and applying it to her life.

Though her family remained about as peaceful as the stock car races, Cynthia recognized that she could not ignore her family and still claim to love God. So she found a safe place to land and then inched forward on the long journey toward forgiveness.

She forgave her father, who'd been sober for almost none of her life or memory. She forgave him for his violence, his absence, and his unfaithfulness to her mother and to her and her siblings. On the most joyous day of her young life, her wedding day, her daddy walked her down the aisle, clean and sober for the first time since she'd known him. A wedding-day gift, radiantly received, painfully given.

With such a difficult childhood home, Cynthia's marriage should have failed. Her children should be disasters. She should be sitting in a corner buzzing her lips, her thoughts swirling in hazy circles of anger and pain.

But not Cynthia. From her vantage point of healing and hope, she gathered young women under her wing, mentored them, and taught them through example of the love of God and the forgiveness found in Christ Jesus. She and her husband worked steadily at their marriage and refused to replicate the chaos she experienced growing up. Their children grew up in a home where love and grace lived, and now they too love God and their spouses with an unending love. Cynthia speaks around the world, with many books to her credit, but she only smiles and laughs and points to God. Only by God's grace, only because Christ saved her.

Her life is more magnificent than she could have ever dreamed. And still she dreams, God-sized dreams bigger than her imagination. She attributes the work God does through her to that foundational work of forgiveness that began as a teenager when she walked down the aisle toward life and love. Every time an ugly memory surfaces or a wound reactivates—and of course they do, opportunities abound for unforgiveness and pain to rule the day—she stops and deliberately forgives.

Dream come true? Absolutely. Because Cynthia believes that God's love trumped all pain and chooses to live accordingly. To live forgiving.

TRAVELING MERCY

Dear one,
Love trumps pain.
Forgiveness trumps the past.
Live into it,
Dear one,
So you can really live.
Otherwise the pain wins,
The ugliness wins,
And the world loses out
On what I can do
Through one person
Who chooses to live
Free.

NOTE TO SELF

Dreams live when I forgive.

DREAM RELIEF

"Tell me your dreams."

—GENESIS 40:8

In Egypt, dream manuals helped the sages interpret dreams, because, evidently, their plethora of gods couldn't and needed to leave something for the human beings to do. Typical dream elements were catalogued and explained. The sages then consulted the manuals and offered an interpretation.

Joseph wouldn't have had access to those dream manuals while in prison. And his response when the cupbearer and the baker shared their dreams issued a clear statement about God: "Do not interpretations belong to God?" (Gen. 40:8). In other words, no one reads a book to find out what a dream means. If God speaks through dreams, then God will also interpret those dreams.

But Joseph's words also reveal more about his own relationship with God. He withstood the advances of Potiphar's wife when he declared, "How then could I do such a wicked thing and sin against God?" (Gen. 39:9). We witnessed his integrity and servant attitude as coming from God, although he hadn't verbalized that himself. And now

he said, "Tell me your dreams," as though he had access to
God's mind, to God's thoughts and reasons behind the
dreams. A huge, risky, potentially dangerous move on
Joseph's part, like a bragging and swaggering inmate, pre-
suming to know God's designs behind dreams. If he was
wrong, his number just might be up and he'd become yet
another prison statistic.

"Tell me yours dreams," he encouraged the baker and the
cupbearer, though telling his dreams to his own brothers
landed him in slavery and then in prison, and even though his
life was so far from his own initial dream. Where does such
courage originate? How, in that prison, did Joseph dare to
invite others to verbalize their dreams?

As far as we know, Joseph's own dreams hadn't been fully
explained to him. And he did not realize that their fulfillment
waited around the corner, ready to unfold beyond his wildest
imagination.

And perhaps because his own brothers turned against him
when he shared his dreams, he found the courage to honor
others' dreams.

The courage to dream, and to encourage others to dream,
in spite of our own unfulfilled or failed dreams comes from
somewhere outside of us. Or somewhere deeper than us,
some reserve shored up by heaven's resources. Joseph's generosity when he invited the prisoners, "Tell me your dreams,"
speaks of a deep well.

Of course, he likely also kept a close eye on opportunities
to sneak a word to the outside world and the powers that be, so
perhaps he had motives beyond generosity when he encouraged

the prisoners to find relief in telling him their dreams. Joseph wanted out of that prison, however willing he might have been to serve at maximum capacity and humility.

Still, Joseph continued to believe in the power and the possibility of a dream, though he had experienced more of failed dreams than of their fulfillment.

Dreams defy failure. They defy dark prison cells. They stand against the thick stone barriers of mockery and risk. Dreams shout against the bleakest of night and shine hope into despair. Dreams sneak in between the steel bars of loss and false accusations. They rob pain of its incapacitating power. Dreams stalk straight through the walls of fear.

Joseph didn't have the faintest idea what dreams his fellow prisoners would share. But he knew, beyond the shadows of doubt that darkened those prison walls, the God of dreams. He knew, as he etched scratches day after long day, that the God who initiates dreams is also the God who brings them to pass.

TRAVELING MERCY
Dear one,
You don't need a dream manual.
Tell me your dreams
So together we can battle the darkness.
Shine light in the cell of despair.
Don't be afraid to dream,
And don't be afraid to tell me
Your dreams.

NOTE TO SELF
Cooperating with dreams is my responsibility;
fulfilling them is God's.

OCTOBER 15

BAD DREAMS

"Do not interpretations belong to God? Tell me your dreams."

—GENESIS 40:8

Not all dreams, of course, are prophetic. At least, I hope not. During deadline drama, some of my writer friends and I have "sick baby" dreams: Our babies are ill, we can't find them, we can't take care of them, they're dying, they're ugly, no one loves them, and we are colossal failures as parents. (The sick baby, in case you didn't catch it, is the current writing project.)

My speaker version of these professional dreams includes, for instance, the one this morning, which played itself out in between me hitting the snooze button for two solid hours. After being invited to speak on Israel (I am writing about Abraham, Isaac, Jacob, Joseph, and all their contemporaries), I showed up without a single PowerPoint slide, without my notes. Because of a strange room layout, some of the people actually were seated around the corner. And no one thought to give me a microphone, which meant that no one could hear me. This might have been a good thing, because evidently I also had absolutely nothing to say to this group of people.

Thankfully, I woke up, sweating like I'd just left a hot yoga class (in which I have never participated, also thankfully—speaking of nightmares).

Dreams spy on our deepest anxieties and then report them back to our conscious mind. If we can remember them in the morning, and if we pay attention, we can learn where we carry worry or fear. Dreams like this offer us hope. We can turn them over to the One who catches us when we fall and inspires our dreams in the first place.

Not that those awful elements would come true, but in a sense, these dreams are actually prophetic. Though it's counterintuitive, often fear is one of the signs that we are called to a particular gifting or endeavor. So when we writers and speakers have "failure" dreams about our profession, we find comfort in God's sufficiency. God, after all, calls us to use our gifts, and since God is the God of the impossible, then it's reasonable that our gifts come with our own impossibles and God's possibles. So fear in this dream scenario confirms our gifts while also handing us over to God.

Whether we dream with our eyes open or closed, we still choose to trust the author of our faith and the biggest dreamer ever. If God can dream up such glory in creation, if God can dream *us*, may the dreams he plants in us root, grow, bloom, and bear fruit.

Wake up. This is the real thing, the real life, the real dream. Let's trust God, rub the sleep from our eyes, and live it.

TRAVELING MERCY

Dear one,
Time to wake up,
Sleepyhead.
And your dream
Really was a dream,
Though it seemed to be
A nightmare in part,
Because it highlights your fear.
Bring that fear.
Come here to me,
And together we will see
What impossible looks like
Lived out in this world.
Keep dreaming with your eyes
Wide open.

NOTE TO SELF

Fear is natural, but God is bigger.

A RISKY BUSINESS

When [one] makes a vow to the LORD or takes an oath to
obligate himself by a pledge, he must not break his
word but must do everything he said.

—NUMBERS 30:2

Dreams are risky for us because they just may be telling
us to orchestrate a change in our lives, to listen to submerged
longings or neglected giftings.

When my husband and I were fairly fresh to ministry, God
kept elbowing me in the ribs to pursue writing. The healthier I
grew emotionally, the more vivid the longing to write became.
But as a pastor's wife, I offered my time and love and minimal
gifts wherever needed, and in particular felt called to help
my husband with the overwhelming responsibilities of the
pastorate.

But the more I helped, the more opportunities to help
materialized, because ministry is an ever-expanding stream
of needs and demands. At one point, when I was invited to
chaperone a youth mission trip, I couldn't get around the
logistics, childcare of our two small children being one of the
enormous issues. But more than the logistics was this dream
that sat on my chest every single day: "What if you write?" it
whispered. "You should be writing."

I needed to say no to the trip, but fear of disappointing the crew of volunteers ate away at me. That night, I dreamed of a road that petered down to a lane. Then huge potholes diverted the lane. Logs rolled in front of my car, house-sized boulders tumbled down the roadside, and I dodged and detoured endlessly. Always, I tried to return to the lane. Around the mountainside I drove and dodged.

When I awoke, I knew. Saying yes to even a good opportunity simply pitched rocks into my path, forcing yet another detour. So saying yes to the dream of writing meant saying no to other ministry opportunities. The more I listened, the more I recognized that I couldn't afford to detour around yet another boulder in the road.

Dreams are risky for the dreamer, too, because our no to one ministry leaves a gap that another must fill. One friend mentioned that after four decades of teaching girls at an after-school Bible study, she needed to resign and let someone else step in. Her health issues made the ministry difficult, and new gifts and callings were emerging for her. She gave a year's notice to the leadership team. The final week of that year, the team leader announced in church that since my friend resigned, the entire program would close down.

Someone asked her, "Do you feel guilty?" My friend answered, "No. To say yes denies another the opportunity to grow in their gifts. And God hasn't called me to this for another year. It's time for me to listen to God and follow in new ways."

When we listen to our dreams and God's calling, people may be disappointed or even blame us. People love our yeses far more than our nos.

We run that risk when we say yes to our dreams. But if saying yes to God means saying no to something less than God's best, we must always say yes to God's best.

TRAVELING MERCY
Dear one,
Yes carries a price tag,
But I already paid it.
Say yes to the best.
Say yes to me,
And I will take care of the rest.
Be gracious in your no,
But do not let others
Press you into their mold,
Into their needs,
Into their own deficits.
There are specific needs your dreams will meet.
Invite others to listen to their own dreams,
And show them the joy of listening to me
And following the dreams I give.

NOTE TO SELF
Yes to God may mean no to others.

WHEN DREAMS WAIT

"I too had a dream."
—GENESIS 40:16

Sometimes dreams send a directive: change something about your life or seek healing in some area. But dreams also can be everything-but-the-kitchen-sink at times, throwing multiple images and ideas and people into the same sphere. They might indicate not just an overcrowding in dreamland, but a lot of unresolved issues or relationships or overwhelming stress.

And then, occasionally, dreams are prophetic, predicting something yet to happen, something beyond your own orchestration. These dreams are particularly telling, because if you speak of them, people watch for their fulfillment. If you interpret them, your head is on the line, perhaps not literally as in Joseph's time but certainly reputationally, then and now. In Old Testament days, people and leaders watched prophets with a raised eyebrow, waiting to see if what they prophesied came true. (And sometimes if they didn't like the dream or the negativity of the prophets, they threw them in prison or in a cistern. Then, as now, people want the good news, not the bad.)

Sometimes, however, an enormous time lag stretches between the prophecy and the fulfillment. Many Scriptures prophesy about the coming Messiah, but those prophets were long dead before their words came true. Meanwhile, the people waited for the fulfillment, unless they got distracted or tired of hanging around checking their watches and the daily birth records in the palaces for the king who would deliver them from darkness and heartbreak.

When Joseph offered the correct interpretation without consulting experts or textbooks, the cupbearer was relieved. Perhaps Joseph spoke the truth. He would be restored to service! What fabulous news for him and his family.

The baker, hearing the cupbearer's good dream report, entrusted his own dream to the imprisoned prophet and fellow dreamer. But the baker's optimism disappeared when he heard the interpretation: he would lose his head and be impaled on a spike. He turned whiter than the fine flour in his dream and hoped against hope that Joseph was wrong.

The proof of Joseph's wisdom was in the interpretations' fulfillment. The cupbearer returned to the palace; the baker lost his head. Within three days, the dreams came true. But for Joseph's own dreams, prophetic though they were, thirteen years passed before Joseph earned the possibility of living into the dream. Thirteen long years to hold on to the dream without giving up, without dashing the dream on the walls of disappointment there in that lonesome prison.

Perhaps for your dreams, years pass without producing fruit. This is true for some of mine, as well, we've welcomed many new years without also welcoming fulfilled dreams.

For us, as likely for Joseph, the dripping sands in the hour-glass force our trust. Not just in the veracity of the dream, but in the God who sends dreams our way. Trusting God's timing, wherever we land in the intervening years, however long we wait, we return to the central truth that the will of God *will* be done in our lives. We trust, we work, we wait, and we cooperate.

TRAVELING MERCY
Dear one,
Your dreams are safe
Because I sent them.
Your head isn't on the line.
Your dreams and the wait
Will help you lean near
To my voice
And hold tightly
To my hand.

NOTE TO SELF
Trust. Work. Wait. Cooperate.

DREAM A DIFFERENCE

Pharaoh had a dream.

—GENESIS 41:1

Abraham had a dream, and he was as good as dead. Isaac had a dream, and he never left the country. Jacob had a dream, and he was a thief. Joseph had a dream, and his brothers hated him. The cupbearer had a dream, and he lived to tell about it. The baker had a dream, but he was in over his head, or without it, turns out. Pharaoh had a dream, and it saved a nation or two.

Dreams matter. However improbable those dreams might be. (A baby at age ninety-nine? Get real!) The power of a dream cannot be argued. Dreams needn't make sense to us or be realistic. A nation of kings and queens from one man with a barren wife? From a second man with a barren wife? From a young man (and also a barren wife)? From a teenager too young to even edit himself? Perhaps the less probable a dream is, the more likely that God waits behind that dream to bring it to fulfillment.

Dreams provide energy, fuel for forward movement. Dreams sustain hope and help ensure our relevance. Without dreams, we begin to die. We see it in churches today. Without a vision for reaching the lost, without a vision for loving our neighbors as ourselves, without a vision for living beyond meetings and beyond reaching our own budgetary needs and keeping the pews polished or the chairs in line, without a vision for holiness, the church becomes irrelevant.

Why not dream? Dream about relevance. Music star Willie Nelson had a dream to raise money for hurting farmers. In 1985 the inaugural Farm Aid concert debut in Illinois raised nine million dollars, and since then has morphed into a large tent covering multiple needs with farmers as the focus. Whatever you think of Willie Nelson, his passion to help farmers is surely akin to Joseph, whose agricultural, business, and leadership sense kept nations alive by wise food storage and distribution.

One of the ways we begin to dream is to look at the needs that surround us.

Feed the hungry? Jesus liked that dream. Concerned about prisoners? That one, too. What about people who need clothes? Check. The sick? You bet. Dream after dream, fulfilled on small and larger scales, all attempting to meet needs that beg for our attention and God's love.

Dream to make a difference, to contribute to fulfilling the needs around us. Hungry people hear the good news of God's love better on a full stomach with the hope of a meal tomorrow, too. Otherwise, where is God, and what is good about starvation?

But when God's people show up with plenty of dreams and the desire to make a difference, the hungry and hurting begin to believe there is good news after all, and it might just pertain to them.

TRAVELING MERCY
Dear one,
Dream on.
Dream a different world,
A world where people are fed and full,
A world where people are safe,
A world where people know
Their worth.
Dream on, dear one.
Dream to make a difference
In small ways
And big ways.
There's good news to share,
And people will believe it
When they see it.

NOTE TO SELF
Needs lead to dreams lead to hope.

WATER FOR THE SOUL

Pharaoh had a dream: He was standing by the Nile.

—GENESIS 41:1

I stood on the bluff that hovers in the sky between Holland, Michigan, and Lake Michigan, with the wind blowing in my face and tears teasing my eyes. I wanted to breathe in the beauty to fill my soul. We clambered down the steep wooden stairs and walked at the water's edge. That evening we raced to the bluff to watch the sun's descent beyond the watery abyss. As glory spread across the sky, my soul wept. Though rains had filled the lake, I lived in a near-drought spiritually. Our move removed us from a spectacular view of sloping greens, giant oaks, and rippling waters to a tightly packed city on the edge of Chicago. We love our location and it is crucial to our ministry life to be here. We rejoice over this amazing opportunity.

But my soul. There alongside Lake Michigan, my soul refused to be silenced about the painful withdrawal from the life support that beauty offers me.

In Pharaoh's dream, he stood above the Nile River, the source of life for Egypt. Looking at a map, a long green band outlines both sides of the river, in high contrast to the dull brown desert beyond the greenery. When the Nile flourishes, Egypt flourishes. When the Nile dries up, Egypt dries up too. Without water, nations plunge into famine. People die. Life cannot exist without water.

Nor can I. If I listen carefully, one language God uses to speak to me is beauty. Beauty allows me to hear God's love. So I consider this: If beauty is one of my soul's love languages, then how will I communicate with God? How will I nourish my heart in this season? And since beauty is my Nile River—it is the translator between my soul and heart and God—well, I must find places that give voice to glory.

Death by spiritual dehydration just won't do.

I have taken to the streets for filling. I walk or jog and pay attention to the beautiful architecture. To the mown lines in a lawn. A man with a nursing assistant leans over his walker and together they move down the sidewalk. His veteran's cap and his kind face spark a smile in me, and we howdy and laugh a moment. I walk onward, moisture pricking my eyes.

In my office on the third floor, I place a straight-back chair that belonged to my grandmother and climb upon it. I open the windows and lean outward, watching the butterfly garden beyond the rooftop and street below. The butterflies are too small for me to see, but the sun-colored coneflowers and the purple wands of bushes wave at me, catching my eye and whispering, "See? Do you hear? God loves you."

When the rains splatter onto the window frames, forcing me to close the leaded glass, I fix my gaze, still, on the portraits through those panes. A corner of green from a towering maple, a puff of white from the clouds, a panel of purple-gray all tell me that God is watering this world.

And watering my soul. If I will but notice and drink. And breathe in. Only then can I breathe out the breath of God into this world.

TRAVELING MERCY
Dear one,
Learn your soul's language,
And then listen.
Listen closely to my voice
Spoken through the wind and the clouds,
The flowers and the trees,
The dimpling of light on water
And the glory of the skylight.
I still speak
And want you to hear
My love.
To hydrate and then fill
To overflowing
In a thirsty world.

NOTE TO SELF
Find a water source. Drink. Share.

MEMORY BLOWOUT

"Today I recall my failures."

—GENESIS 41:9 NET

Pharaoh awakened with a nightmare migraine, his head pounding with detailed dreams—hopeful, menacing, a duo of fat and skinny dreams serious enough for him to holler for help from all the dream-wise people in his entourage. All experts shook their heads and slouched in their chairs in Pharaoh's war room. The dreams defied their understanding and interpretation. The king, ready to fly off the handle, scanned the room with wild eyes.

Ah, but one man, an unlikely sort to consult with people about their dreams, spoke up. The cupbearer swallowed hard and opened his mouth.

"Today I am reminded of my shortcomings," he said (Gen. 41:9). Not only reminded of them, but he spoke of them, even at the risk of looking bad. After all, image is everything if you're the cupbearer. He was Pharaoh's frontline defense, uncovering any attempts at treason or poison. For him to acknowledge any shortcomings could land him in hot water, like, say, prison, with a price on his head like his former colleague the baker.

What courage! Of course we're reminded of our short-comings every single day. Not one day passes where I fail to realize I have failed yet again. And again. My shortcomings far outweigh any accomplishments. I'm well aware of them, but am I going to run to Pharaoh and remind him of my short-comings? Maybe not. Probably not. Especially if my job or my life is at stake.

But the cupbearer's humility combined with courage and a sincere desire, it seems, to help his distraught leader, forced the words from his tongue before he could even censor them. A good thing, it turns out, that he spoke before the editor in him kicked in.

The only other person who knew that Joseph interpreted dreams was now dead.

"I am reminded of my shortcomings." Good thing! When the Holy Spirit reminds of us of our shortcomings, what freedom we find in confessing them. More than freedom, however, acknowledging shortcomings may open the way for God's work to be done in the world. The cupbearer's decision to spill would turn the tide of the entire country.

When the cupbearer remembered that he'd forgotten about Joseph, that he'd gone on with his jolly and important life in Pharaoh's large house, humility struck him. He retold his own story of imprisonment, of Pharaoh's anger with him and the baker, and of their dreams. And then he said, "Now a young Hebrew was there with us, a servant of the captain of the guard" (41:12). (Even though Joseph was a fellow prisoner, the cupbearer respected him as a servant of the official still— a telling reference to Joseph's behavior in prison.)

Pharaoh grasped at the fragile hope his cupbearer offered, with not a word about the man's shortcomings. About the cup-bearer's humility to confess, and his willingness to highlight another's gifts, who would imagine that on such character qualities the fate of nations hinged?

TRAVELING MERCY
Dear one,
Don't be afraid
To share your shortcomings,
To let people in on the secret
Of your failures
When the time seems right.
And don't be afraid
To give others credit,
Even if you look
Different or
Less gifted or wise
Than they.
In a world of people eager to take credit
For themselves and for others
Humility disarms.

NOTE TO SELF
Disarm and dream forward with honesty and humility.

THE RIGHT TIME

Pharaoh sent for Joseph, and he was quickly
brought from the dungeon.

—GENESIS 41:14

When the warden materialized in the grimness of prison at Joseph's shoulder and ordered him to bathe and shave, surely Joseph both grimaced and hoped simultaneously. A shave and a change of clothes must be good news, right? They wouldn't clean him up and then hang him for some trumped-up offense, would they?

So he scraped a blade over his face, scrubbed the prison grime from his body, and slipped with relief into clean clothes. With a deep breath, he headed to meet with Pharaoh. For what purpose, he couldn't imagine.

The tension surrounding Pharaoh shook Joseph. All these bright people, the magicians and wise men of Egypt crowded into the room, sweat beading on their foreheads. And Pharaoh looked like he'd spent the night in a torture chamber. Maybe he had.

Then Joseph saw the cupbearer, the man whose dream he interpreted two years before. For the first time, hope shoved aside Joseph's pervasive prisoner's dread. He stood straight before the king and waited.

"I had a dream, and no one can interpret it. But I have heard it said of you that when you hear a dream you can interpret it," Pharaoh said (Gen. 41:15).

Joseph glanced at the brilliant thinkers in the room. Unlike them, he had no dream manual. "I cannot do it," he answered. Did Pharaoh's eyes turn mad, did he reach for a sword, did the others in the room sound a chorus of gasps? But Joseph wasn't finished. He'd learned a bit about God, after serving so long in nightmare conditions. "I cannot do it . . . but God will give Pharaoh the answer he desires" (41:16).

But wait. What if God doesn't? What if Joseph doesn't understand the dreams at all and God stays silent as a stone? The risk to Joseph just might be losing his head. Besides, what if God gives an answer and it isn't what Pharaoh desires? What then?

The king, relieved, poured out the details of both dreams. The beautiful fat cows, seven of them, sleek and healthy, grazed among the reeds of the Nile River. But then, seven scrawny, hideous, boney cows rose from the river. "I had never seen such ugly cows in all the land of Egypt," Pharaoh said (41:19). Then, horrors! The thin cows gobbled up the beautiful plump cows, but looked every inch as ugly as before.

In the second dream, seven heads of grain sprouted, full, all on a single stalk. Next, seven withered, meager, scorched heads sprouted and devoured the good heads. Pharaoh said, "I told this to my magicians, but none of them could explain it to me" (41:24).

No, magicians had no corner on the market of dream interpretation. But thankfully, God did and God does. And God showed Joseph, who shared with Pharaoh not just the dream, but a solution to navigate the dire prophecy that appeared to Pharaoh in the middle of his restless night and day.

Joseph had toiled for nine years in prison. Two years before, he'd begged the cupbearer to try to secure Joseph's freedom. Yet only on God's timetable, only in God's blueprint would Joseph be freed.

No matter how long we toil, no matter how many alternate routes we seek, no matter how long we wait, God's timing will always be perfect.

TRAVELING MERCY
Dear one,
You tried to find a way out
Of this prison,
But don't forget
I hold the master key
To the dungeon,
And you will be free
One day on my timetable.
Trust me on this.
Don't fail to do your very best,
But wait on my deliverance.
I won't fail you.
I promise.
And you will speak my words
To many.

NOTE TO SELF
Wait. Trust. Seek. Speak.

THE POWER OF A DREAM

"I had a dream."

—GENESIS 41:15

The mug on my window ledge speaks of dreams. Long-ago dreams. Not just my dreams, but the dreams of my mother, who longed to transport her children and grandchildren to another world, a perfect world where imagination meets childhood meets delight.

But the dream began long before that, when a little boy awakened in the middle of the night, night after night, and pulled on thin-soled shoes, little protection against the deep, wet snow outside. He shrugged into a flimsy jacket, hefted a heavy bag of newspapers on his young shoulders, and set out long before little boys should be awake. He returned home, chilled to the bone and with no dry clothes to wear, so he went to school cold, wet, hungry, and exhausted. After school, he repeated the scenario, shivering and pushing through the weather to help contribute to his family's meager income.

But that little boy dreamed of magic, of places of delight and joy where pain disappeared and every single color, sound, and scent spelled *perfect*. Spelled *safety*. Spelled *love*.

That little boy was Walter Elias Disney. He sold his first cartoon during grade school. Once he stood outside an amusement park with his sister and brother. He said as they watched people enter and leave that one day he would own an amusement park. And his would be clean. He dropped out of school at sixteen to fight in World War I, but was rejected by the military because of his age. Instead he drove an ambulance in France for the Red Cross, then returned to America to study art.

Disney started his own animation business with one employee, but bankruptcy shut it down in 1923. He eventually moved to Hollywood with one hundred dollars in his pocket, full of dreams and conviction and with enough passion and talent to survive the ups and downs of the depression, another war, defection by his staff, and stolen works. After Mickey Mouse became a superstar, many other animated and feature films followed. He never lost sight of his dream: to create magic for children and adults, to bring life and laughter to all the little Walts in the world.

Postponed due to WWII, the dream grew from an eight-acre park for employees to a 160-acre, seventeen-million-dollar site in Orange County, California. Disneyland opened in 1955, in a one-hundred-degree heat wave, with hot asphalt trapping women's heels, a plumbers' strike, and fountains not working. Yet his dream lives on and has enchanted the lives of over 650 million people since it opened.

A man and a mouse? No kidding. The power of a dream and the courage to follow that dream. To stay focused, to refuse to lose to failure, to choose to bounce back from disappointment: the elements of a dream. Not only did he survive a difficult childhood, he drew from that pain a determination to bring joy to others.

The mug on my window ledge with its mouse silhouette and memories of my mother's dream trip for us reminds me to dream, determine, focus, and follow.

TRAVELING MERCY

Dear one,
You may not own a mega-company,
May never be rich or famous.
But look at what you lack,
And decide how you can build on those deficits
From your past or your present
To make a difference in people's lives
In the future.
A man and a mouse?
How about you
And the God of the universe?
I think we have a match
Made in heaven.

NOTE TO SELF

Dream. Determine. Focus. Follow.

THE FAITH OF YES AND NO

"God will give Pharaoh the answer he desires."

—Genesis 41:16

Joseph never claimed to have the power to interpret dreams, but rather trusted God to teach him the truth of those dreams. He told Pharaoh, "I cannot do it, but God will give Pharaoh the answer he desires."

The answer Pharaoh desired? Well, yes and no. Pharaoh wanted an answer to the mystery of the dreams, but Pharaoh surely didn't desire this dream in its entirety. Fat cows and fat grain, yes, bring them on. Famine to follow? No. Not on the royal menu.

Isn't this true for us? We cannot interpret our lives and our dreams or anyone else's for that matter; not always, maybe never, and rarely with any amount of certainty in advance. Retrospect does offer some clarity, but it's called perspective rather than prophecy.

Consider, though, the times you've expected God to give you the answer you desired. Usually we expect a positive outcome, a good spin on a difficult place or an even better outcome from a currently good spot. When we pray, we aren't asking

God to do the worst in our lives. We're asking for God's best. This is where prayer becomes tricky and faith sometimes prickly to sustain. We pray in hope, but we don't always receive in relief, getting the results we prayed for. We pray in hope, and hopefully we release the decision-making to God. Sometimes we chew our fingernails of faith down to the quick while we wait, worrying about less-than-desired results.

Will the prodigal come home? The unemployment end? The diagnosis clear? The marriage be saved? A loved one be spared?

"God will give Pharaoh the answer he desires." Not a lush and lovely answer, not by far. And so it is with us, as well. It's true we want an answer, but we want the answer we want. The feast without the famine would be super nice and comfy, and we would be happy, happy, happy all the time.

But God answers our desires in ways that mesh with heavenly purposes. We will always receive our answers. They just may not be ones we personally endorsed beforehand. The answer may be "wait." Wait for a little while, wait for a long while, wait until heaven. The heavenly response might be a resounding no with accompanying door slam. No to that job. No to that relationship. No to that clean bill of health.

These answers are difficult to live with. It's difficult to sustain faith in their midst. If God is good, why don't we get the answers we want? Now or eventually?

Looking at Pharaoh's yes/no, good/bad dream, we know the results. The feasting season (Yahoo! Yes! Fabulous!) allowed the country to prosper and prepare for the fasting season, and so the yes prepared the way for the no. The same is true for us. But we don't see the end from the beginning, don't know how the current yes will help us in the next no, don't know if we now live in the no after having lived in the yes.

But a no here, remember, opens the door for a yes elsewhere.

TRAVELING MERCY
Dear one,
Will you live in my no
And in my yes,
Trusting me that yes
Prepares you to save up
For the no,
And that no
Allows you to anticipate the yes
Coming around the bend?
Will you trust me enough
To live in this place,
This yes and no,
This now and not yet
Place of faith,
Knowing that my desire for you
Is to know my love
And live in that love,
Loving others all the way through?
However that looks,
It's plenty of yes
For now.

NOTE TO SELF
Trust the yes and no for they are vital
ingredients for dream living.

A REAL GOOD DREAM

Seven years of great abundance are coming
throughout the land of Egypt.

—Genesis 41:29

Running roughly 4,200 miles throughout the length of Egypt, the Nile River is the country's lifeblood and lifeline. The Nile provides the primary water supply for both Egypt and modern-day Sudan with multiple other countries sharing its resources. The river stretches most of the continent's length, flows northward through the Sudanese desert and through Egypt to a wide delta, then empties into the Mediterranean Sea. Nearly half of Egypt's population lives in the Nile Delta region.

The Nile River's levels determined the affluence of the people and the entire country. Fat cows, fat heads of grain? Pharaoh rubbed his hands together. Seven years of riches. Water led to plump grains which led to beefy cattle which led to economic growth and likely taxes, too. So far Pharaoh loved this dream, the dream of many rulers. Riches. Prosperity. Luxury. Style. And popularity: People love leaders who link them to times of fortune.

Then again, wisdom in the midst of prosperity requires discipline. Spending the excess feels fabulous and tempting, and also like it's something deserved for years of work. "Live it up, spend it fast, you earned it," our shortsighted soul suggests.

Except in this instance, the seven years of flourishing land and fields, of crops and flocks—Pharaoh and his citizens couldn't take credit for them. Farmers make wise choices but they can't control the weather, and when the weather is favorable, they roll with those blessings. Seven years of great abundance? Hallelujah. Bale the hay, store it away, and climb back on that tractor and plant more grain today, because you don't know what tomorrow brings.

Once when speaking in northern North Dakota during the economic downturn after 2008, I mentioned the difficulty of the recession. The women looked at me kindly but also without comprehending, as though I suddenly spoke in a foreign tongue. "We haven't felt it here," they said. "We're an agricultural society. We're careful with our resources."

We could use a little of that wisdom in times of feasting and times of famine. Stewardship. Regulating our own spending and our savings. As Joseph would demonstrate, the more we save, the more we have to spare and the more we can share. *Save*. Not a word spoken freely in churches today.

Then what if, in our plenty or in our poverty, we remember to pray, "Lord, bless the hands that feed us"? And we include the farmers, who live by faith every single day of their lives? How about we include everyone along the way who deals with that food, from the picker to the driver, to the warehouse worker, to the market clerk, to the person in your home who prepares that food (and add in the manufacturer if you don't eat whole foods)? A long line of blessings.

And remember the rule we learned in kindergarten: "Don't forget to share."

TRAVELING MERCY

Dear one,
I bless from heaven
And provide food for you daily.
Be wise with all I give you.
Save for a rainy day,
And share with those in need.
I dream of a time
When hunger and thirst
Are no more.
Give beyond yourself,
And I will bless from my bounty.
It's all part of the dream.

NOTE TO SELF

Sanctify. Save. Share.

FEAST TIMES

"Seven years of great abundance are coming."
—GENESIS 41:29

The secret to living well in the feast times? Recognize them, for starters. Only in retrospect did I realize how wonderful our last home was. Most of it, 97.5 percent of it, I absolutely loved. I feasted daily on the beautiful views, visually caressed every bloom on the lilac in spring and the brilliant mums and sedum in the fall, and reveled in the fiery colors of leaves like giants' bouquets on the tall trees. Recognizing beauty while in its midst is a great means of feasting.

Still, I secretly (or not so secretly) wanted a new kitchen, or a newer one, as unrealistic and ridiculous and shallow though such longings may be or are, in fact. Really, that was about the extent of my wish list in that house. The kitchen became charming, once we put in some elbow grease and significant sweat in one-hundred degree weather, and added new paint and new vision into decorating it, tearing out a hideous, or at least severely dated, bench system that we inherited. I loved the improvements. But inside the whisper, "New countertops, redesigned space . . ." That little longing poked at me. Now, with the eyes of perspective, I realize how unusual those cabinets were, how tall and deep. I wish I'd loved all of it more than I allowed myself. Wish I'd noticed what we had rather than longed for what we did not have.

Choosing gratefulness is a good way to live well, wherever we find ourselves.

I'm embarrassed to admit that even though I frequently noticed the beauty of daily life like the turtle lumbering its way across the yard and leaving a wide imprint in the dewy green grass; even though I loved hearing neighborhood children chattering as they giggled their way down the hill on skateboards and bikes; even though I thanked God for all these, still the single element that sliced through the joy was worry. I worried with vague, wordless worry or with very wordy worry. What a thief. We don't live well in feast times (or famine either) with worry constantly on our mind. Worry robs the marrow from the bones of our faith.

But the answer to worry? It's still the same remedy: gratitude. To stuff ourselves so full of gratitude that it crowds out all the worry demons.

Store up the good. Fill yourself to overflowing with joy and beautiful memories. With the sound of laughter and the running feet of happiness. Every day might not be Thanksgiving, but every day there are morsels for feasting, to stuff into the cheeks of our remembrances.

Praise isn't about what we don't have, not entirely, although we can find ways to praise in the have-not phases. Praise is about noticing what and who we have: the God of all the earth, loving us, providing for us, and inviting us to see and rejoice.

Life is good. God is good. No matter what happens. The sky is blue and the wind is sweet. Flowers bloom. We have food to eat and clothes on our backs and people who love us. We have words to write and music to sing and people to love. Color us happy. Color us full. Color us grateful.

TRAVELING MERCY
Dear one,
Today
Notice the colors.
Notice the laughter, the happy.
Ring the bells of praise.
Sing the notes aloud.
I love it
When you color.

NOTE TO SELF
Find crayons. Color life with gratitude.

DREAMS THAT MAKE A DIFFERENCE

I want you to stress these things, so that those who
have trusted in God may be careful to devote
themselves to doing what is good.

—TITUS 3:8

Had Joseph tried to make his own dream come true, he might have gotten seriously sidetracked by vainglory (I love that old word). His dream of his brothers bowing down to him, without a really good reason for that to happen, could have been dangerous if he sought its fulfillment himself. Forcing people to bow down becomes abuse before too long. Rather, thirteen years of seasoning, maturing, learning, growing, and serving would pass before Joseph was in any position to withstand the trials of having people bow down to him.

They would, in fact, bow down to him, but not because of coercion on Joseph's part. His brothers and an entire country of people would bow. The beautiful truth is that his dream then made a difference. His dream wasn't about himself. The dream was about a dying world. Joseph would be behind an effort that saved nations from destruction and annihilation from famine. Self-fulfilled, his dream would have harmed. God-expanded and God-fulfilled, his dream brought salvation.

Those dreams make a difference. Four-year-old Alexandra Scott determined that when she left the hospital after treatment for neuroblastoma, she would open a lemonade stand. She wanted to make a little difference, not for her own wants or little-girl wishes, but to give money back to her doctors. To help other children with childhood cancer. Her first stand raised two thousand dollars. Her efforts toward a larger good captured the imagination of a nation. Word spread and by her death in 2008, Alex's Lemonade Stand Foundation, through stands and donations across the country, had raised over one million dollars for cancer research. The legacy continues, inspiring people to dream little dreams that make a difference. You never know when they will become big dreams that make a big difference.

So as we dream—as we begin to listen to the still, small voice within that whispers, "Try this; wouldn't you love to . . . ?"—we look beyond the *want* of the dream to the *what* of the dream. What difference will this make? How can God make a difference in this world as a result of us moving toward these dreams?

Whether it's to play ball or play the piano, to make people laugh or to invent a product to make people's lives easier. Whether it's turning T-shirts into dresses for children in wounded countries, recycling prom dresses for underserved young women, or repairing cars for widows as a ministry through the church. Whether it's improving people's life skills or offering education and training to help people break out of poverty. What's your dream? Can you commit that dream to God and invite him to take that dream and make a difference in this world?

Because ultimately, our dreams are not about us, about us making money or a name for ourselves. Though neither is bad, both are shortsighted. We don't want to shortchange what God can do. Our dreams, inspired and gifted by God, become the means for God making a difference in this world.

It's not too late to dream dreams. Finding our promise leads to finding our name, which leads to finding our dream, which leads to finding our way, our mission in this world. Dream little, dream big, dream God-sized dreams. Dream and dare to make a difference. Joseph would be pleased.

TRAVELING MERCY
Dear one,
God-sized dreams
Make a difference.
It's impossible on your own.
Or it's possible but not with the results
We will see together.
With me all things are possible,
So commit your dream to me.
Let's see how one person's dream
Can help offer
Life,
Love,
Laughter,
Hope.
Help.
We can do this.
So dream on.

NOTE TO SELF
Dream to make a difference starting today.

MVP IN THE DREAM ROOM

"Can we find anyone like this man?"

—Genesis 41:38

Without asking, "Do you want the good news or the bad news first?" Joseph laid out the interpretation of Pharaoh's double dream. But the king didn't even have time to wring his hands in despair because in the next breath Joseph offered a way through the next fourteen years. With careful planning, the seven years of plenty would see the country through the seven years of famine.

Joseph didn't just throw water on the dream interpretation party; he threw in a solution. It all happened so quickly that we can't chalk it up simply to business acumen and political savvy. OK, so Joseph's instant solution came from the combination of thirty years' experience in agriculture as well as in accounting and field management for Potiphar. But for the plan to unfold in such an instantaneous manner? Joseph listened deeply to the dream. That level of listening requires both faith and emotional maturity.

People abound who will listen to a dream and then dash it onto the hard rocks of reality with every conceivable problem or drawback. But listening to a dream and determining a course of action requires brain training and being people savvy. It seems that, during Joseph's thirteen-year tenure of servitude, he learned more than just a foreign language and accounting with some fieldwork thrown in. He acquired emotional intelligence, a valuable characteristic in both the marketplace and the throne room.

In the middle of a tension-riddled hall, rife with worry and fear and a bunch of Pharaoh-pleasing false prophets and seers, Joseph could have seriously blundered. With the pressure of his long years of servitude riding on his shoulders, his desire to get out of prison through this one big chance at Pharaoh's favor could have jettisoned the opportunity. Anger at the cupbearer for forgetting him could have tripped him on his journey forward.

But Joseph grew in faith and in emotional maturity and intelligence during his tenure. These strengths kept him from being sidetracked by the high stakes of the court, by the dream's frightening reading, and by the king's favor. He kept his head (in all ways) and spoke with wisdom and discernment.

"And now let Pharaoh look for a discerning and wise man and put him in charge of the land of Egypt," Joseph said (Gen. 41:33). Whether he angled for the position or not isn't clear from the text, but because Joseph developed a credible plan on the spot—demonstrating the very traits Joseph considered necessary—Pharaoh didn't need to look far for such a contender. "Can we find anyone like this man?" he asked, wide-eyed. Pharaoh didn't need a bunch of yes-people, bowing, scrapping reality, and placating him. He needed the reality *and* he needed a good plan.

Joseph's plan made sense to all those present, and the king fast-tracked him from prison to palace. He appointed Joseph as his right hand, second in power only to the king of Egypt.

After his years of disappointment, when his moment arrived, Joseph had all the pieces in place: faith, wisdom, and emotional intelligence. To see the possibility rather than only the problem is the mark of both a dreamer and doer.

So pull out those dreams. Craft a plan. Be realistic and full of faith. And watch God work.

TRAVELING MERCY
Dear one,
Life is full of good-news/bad-news scenarios
And bad-news people.
But when you have a plan,
You can withstand
And work around the bad
To get to the good.
Craft your plan,
Bring it to me,
Dream it,
Learn from your life
And others' around you.
Then plan and grow into
That dream.

NOTE TO SELF
Plan around problems with possibilities.

THE QUIET PRESENCE

So Pharaoh asked his servants, "Can we find anyone
like this—a man who has God's Spirit in him?"

—Genesis 41:38 GW

She waited in line at my favorite grocery store.[1] I loaded my cart's contents onto the conveyer belt while hers started to disappear into her emptied cart to bag herself.

A little logjam occurred when her eggs and milk and small items crammed together. They dislocated the divider we'd placed between our groceries. I repaired the breach and waited for the last of her goods to slide over the scanner and plop into her basket.

"Cash back?" the cashier asked. I finally looked at the shopper. Something instantly warmed me. She shook her head and pressed in her pin number. I looked at her again.

Ordinary clothes—loose jeans and a pink cardigan—cloaked her frame. I glanced toward her face. Soft brown hair fluffed around the gentlest countenance. She didn't really speak to the cashier, at least not while I was within earshot.

But her presence. Her very presence spread comfort and kindness and peace. I looked at her eyes as she reached for the receipt. Her eyes looked wide and alive with interest. I wanted to smile a little more, act a little more loving around her.

My turn next, my almost-belongings dropping into the next empty cart. I met the cashier's eyes, smiled at her, cheered out loud at the low register total in spite of the good amount of groceries purchased. I shoved the basket through the sliding doors toward my car with a smile that I actually felt in my eyes.

Boxes stowed, cart returned, I jumped into my car, off to pick up a waiting child for dinner. Pulling to the edge of the parking lot, I saw the woman with the presence ahead of me, in her minivan. Then I noticed her bumper sticker: "God is wonderful."

Then I really smiled. Aha! That sweet, kind, patient, interested, winsome-without-a-word presence was God. Even now, I smile to think about her. I recognized Christ through her, even before I could give him a name.

I grew up intoning the Lord's Prayer—in unison—during church after the pastoral prayer. How rote my recitation of "Thy kingdom come, Thy will be done." At the grocery store, I knew the coming of God's kingdom in a new way. It visited through one gentle woman's demeanor—not even her words. She wasn't preaching, wasn't reciting Scripture to bored or tuned-out ears, and wasn't spouting "Be blessed" spiritual words. Her love for God, and God's love for her, showed up on her face and transformed her countenance and her attitude.

How like Joseph. This is the presence Potiphar, the prison warden, the prisoners, and Pharaoh all recognized in Joseph throughout his tenure in their service. The word in Hebrew for God is *Ruach Elohim* in Genesis 41:38, meaning "breath or Spirit." A fitting word picture for the filling of Joseph. And the woman in the grocery store.

Even without words, the presence of God enters, breathing into and infiltrating this world with surprising kindness. Such a becoming characteristic. Such a subtle means of inviting others into the winsomeness of God's love.

It occurred to me, much later: I wonder if she sensed God's lovingkindness in me.

TRAVELING MERCY

Dear one,
The world is hurting,
Hurried,
And often angry.
People can use a little kindness,
An honest smile,
A friendly look into their eyes.
Not a hard job description,
But one that beckons others
Toward my love in you.
It's the biggest dream I've ever had,
Loving people
Into heaven.

NOTE TO SELF

Preach love in action.

NOTE

1. A portion of this devotional first appeared as "Thy Kingdom Come," *indeed*, November/December 2009, 9–10.

REMEMBER HOPE

"All the abundance in Egypt will be forgotten. . . .
The abundance in the land will not be remembered."

—GENESIS 41:30–31

When the Scriptures tell us that the seven years of abundance would be forgotten and then, in case we didn't get it the first time, that the people would not remember the years of abundance, well . . . we sit up and listen. The double emphasis is doubly serious. This is grave to forget entirely. Forget all the lushness? All the grain, filling the fields and reaching toward the skies, spilling out of the storehouses? Seven years of green, of outrageous growth, all entirely forgotten?

As Joseph interprets Pharaoh's dream, the seven years of famine spell out a disaster larger than lack of food. Memory is critical, as an individual and as a country. You can't live on the calorie content of memories, but conversely, memories can help you stay alive. Memories are a memento of your journey, and historical amnesia wipes out your travel diaries and the map of where you've been. Things you need to continue on.

The loss of those memories predicted the loss of hope for an entire country. Hope is fuel. Even without calorie content, memories provide fuel for the future. In a World War II concentration camp, prisoners whiled away long hours talking about the meals their mothers or wives prepared. They savored the recipes, every ingredient. They replayed eloquent memories of the aromas and the groaning platters. They held imaginary cooking contests to decide which cook and which meal won. They spun stories around the food and filled themselves with the memory of happy times and of full stomachs. Even though they wasted away to skeletal state, these prisoners focused their minds on their memories. In some critical way, the memory-keeping helped them through the days and kept them looking toward the future when daily bread was once again a fact and not a figment of fantasy.

"The famine will ravage the land," reads Genesis 41:30. The root word for *ravage* in Hebrew means "to finish, to destroy, to bring an end to." This famine would annihilate the country of Egypt. It would be so destructive that it would obliterate even the memory of happier times, times of plenty and bounty.

To lose their memories of the abundance is like telling people they have no past. Forgetting plunges us into a state of anonymity and hopelessness, because then we have no track record of our own journey. And worse, no record of who God has been in our lives.

Without memory, the fearfulness of having no past gives voice to the haunting dread of having no future. Perhaps this is why throughout the Scriptures we're admonished to remember and to not forget. Hundreds of times the verbs are used. Remembering, as seen in the concentration camps, becomes a community discipline, calling out faith to one another because of God's faithfulness in the past.

Regardless of the severity of the famine in our lives, we remember and remind others to not forget: God was faithful yesterday. God will be faithful tomorrow. And today.

TRAVELING MERCY
Dear one,
I have food that others do not know,
So come to me.
Remember the plenty
Of times past,
Even just yesterday
And this morning, too.
And don't forget,
I will not forsake you.
The facts of the famine
Do not equal
A heart full of faith.
So hold on,
Relief is coming.
Remember,
And do not forget.

NOTE TO SELF
Don't forget: God provided yesterday and will
follow through tomorrow.

DREAM TEAMMATES

"And now let Pharaoh look for a discerning and wise man."

—Genesis 41:33

As I rushed through the Houston airport toward my gate, a company's advertisement on a monitor flashed for attention. "The only thing more powerful than a dream?" it asked. "The people who will implement the dream." In other words, get a team. Preferably by hiring the company with the paid advertising spot.

Various advertising and rah-rah motivational speakers and posters herald the wisdom of a team. But teamwork started long before design-your-own-success companies came into being. When creating the universe, God created Adam and then said, "It is not good for the man to be alone" (Gen. 2:18). Then God created Eve, who would become Adam's teammate and helpmate. This didn't always turn out particularly well, but the premise is true through the centuries: It is not good to be alone.

Throughout the Scriptures, example after example supports the idea of teamwork, of companions on the journey. Joseph became Pharaoh's second in command and implemented a monumental dream of survival for civilization. Generations later, God brought Aaron and Miriam alongside Moses, and then Moses included Joshua in his leadership training course. Under Moses' tutelage, Joshua emerged as a mighty leader. He brought Caleb alongside him when the Israelites entered the Promised Land, thus training up yet another champion.

Skip ahead a few hundred years to Jesus. As soon as he exited the wilderness after his baptism by John, Jesus formed a team of disciples and followers. That team would become our team, the company of the saints who would brave the journey of faith for all of us.

Traveling companions keep us moving forward, toward our dreams. When I began trying to craft words into articles, I sought out people to voyage with me. A small group of women who also heard that voice say, "Write this down" joined me, and for more than two decades we have supported each other in this calling. Together we've kept one another writing as we encourage, challenge, and redirect one another. Before we started meeting, none of us had seen anything published. Now, we have together published over forty books and hundreds of articles. As other dreams presented themselves, God allowed me to find other teams to challenge me in my roles as a woman, wife, mother, writer, speaker, and Christ-follower.

Isn't this the basis of Hebrews 10:24–25? "Let us consider how we may spur one another on toward love and good deeds, not giving up meeting together . . . but encouraging one another."

How do you find a team to forward your own dream? Ask God for direction, and keep your eyes open. Look for people with some mileage on their own dreams, some tread on their faith. Seek out people smarter than you, with more or different life experiences. Take a course and watch for the curve-breaker, the person at the top of the class, and tag along. Enroll in a discipleship course or Bible study at church. Find a life coach, a spiritual director. Someone to tutor you further along the road toward holiness and toward dream achievement.

Companions on the journey. That, too, is a dream come true.

TRAVELING MERCY
Dear one,
We partner together
On this route
Toward heaven.
But you need some earthly companions.
So find a team,
Some wise and discerning people,
And learn to spur
One another on toward
Growth and godliness.
And dreams will come true.

NOTE TO SELF
Power the dream; find a team.

LIVING TOWARD THE DREAM

"I hereby put you in charge of the whole land of Egypt."

—GENESIS 41:41

Though Joseph likely didn't realize it, listening to and interpreting the cupbearer's dream and the baker's nightmare put him in line for his own dream's fulfillment. Two years later, when Pharaoh brought him out of prison and put him on the Dream Team for the "Feast and Famine" project, the king's dream would play directly into Joseph's own dream fulfillment from years before.

If Joseph spent much time wondering about his dream as a seventeen-year-old, if he stopped to consider his own path in the intervening years, he surely began to wonder if he'd missed some signs along the way. He'd been stripped of his colorful coat, thrown into a cistern, sold as a slave, and marketed on the auction block to a leader in Egypt. He'd been falsely charged and tossed into prison. He said yes to the dream and ended up in shackles. This is no one's first choice for living the dream.

But in that prison, Joseph paid attention. He noticed the cupbearer and his sadness. He noticed the baker's dejection. He read their feelings displayed on their faces and cared enough to ask, "Why do you look so sad today?" (Gen. 40:7). Though they were important people in Pharaoh's employ (food and wine safety being paramount to survival for kings since meals were easily poisoned), Joseph himself had no reason to reach out to them. He couldn't imagine that their dreams would become the turning point for his own.

Or that those dreams would lead to an audience with the king, who had his own set of troubling dreams.

Or that being part of those dreams' interpretation and implementation would actually lead Joseph straight into his own long-ago dream. All these years of serving, he'd carefully tended the people before him, becoming a vessel God employed in the most unlikely situations. Joseph lived life as a clear witness to God's presence and provision; nine times the Scriptures speak of God's presence and favor through Joseph. Joseph's words in critical moments—with Potiphar's wife, the fellow prisoners, and Pharaoh—tell us that Joseph deferred to God's wisdom and not his own. By being faithful to God in the worst of situations and by caring about others and helping them with their dreams, Joseph's own dream came true.

How shortsighted to focus only on our own dreams and their fulfillment. How much better to enable others' dreams through care, listening, and seeking God's wisdom. In our desperation for the next step, in our longing for God's best, and in our desire for deliverance from our own pits and prisons, we don't mind rushing past the people asking for insight along our path. Perhaps we don't even notice them as we hurry onward, always watching for the person who we think will help *our* dreams come true.

But Joseph lived the opposite way. He served and any favor he received was due entirely to God's presence and blessing over him. Not because he conned his way to the next stepping-stone, but because he noticed and cared. He was faithful in the small things.

That faithfulness put him in line for the big things, the big dream, God saved up for him.

TRAVELING MERCY
Dear one,
Faithfulness in the small things
Creates readiness for the larger things,
Or at least the next things.
Serve as you go.
Notice others' dreams.
Bless them with your presence
And favor.
And see if I don't bless you
En route to your own dream.
Besides,
Serving today
Is part of living the dream
Today
And tomorrow.

NOTE TO SELF
Honor others' dreams. Be part of their team.

NOVEMBER DEVOTIONS

WARDROBING

He dressed him in robes of fine linen and put
a gold chain around his neck.

—GENESIS 41:42

Joseph's wardrobe of coats. Long gone was the amazing, gorgeous, richly ornamented, and conflicted coat of his youth, now bloodstained and shredded, and only a painful memory in Joseph's mind. That cloak, such a symbol of his father's misguided favoritism and its painful repercussions on a family. The coat represented innocence lost and all that is difficult about the generosity and danger of dreams.

His childhood cloak led Joseph to a pit. But the pit? A necessary step toward a dream. Without that coat, Joseph might never have landed in an Egyptian prison.

And then there's the incriminating cloak clutched in the claws of Potiphar's wife, supposed evidence of Joseph's dishonorable intentions. Once again, we see that a coat in the wrong person's hands becomes fodder for mischief if not outright evil. And yet that coat, too, would lead Joseph into the next stage toward the fulfillment of his dream.

That abandoned and troublesome coat landed Joseph in prison, which was precisely where he needed to be in order to hone the skills of dream interpretation, service, and compassion. Just the right timing and he would be called, clean, shaven, and in new clothes, out of prison to the king's palace.

There, with his council's approval, Pharaoh placed Joseph in royal employ, conferring a status on him surpassed only by Pharaoh himself. And now released from prison, Joseph donned the royal clothing suitable to Pharaoh's right hand. The king exchanged Joseph's cheap and coarse prison wear for a new coat, robing him in majestic garments of fine linen.

Isn't this true for us as well? Our covering is shredded, torn, and bloody. It's landed us in both cistern and prison, and it has sold us out as slaves on a chain gang toiling for a cruel master in the quarries of the world. People have stolen our innocence, accused us falsely, and used us maliciously. We've been misjudged and shamed, all the while knowing that our core is seriously flawed.

Don't we all deserve prison, in reality? All of our costuming, our pretense, our troublemaking coverings only disguise the truth. And yet, because of God's work through Christ, we have been released from our debtor's prison and can shed our orange uniforms of shame. Though once captive to our sin, we're set free. Not because we interpret dreams, but because we *are* the dream. God's dream. God wraps us in forgiveness and cloaks us with love from eternity. Exchanging our blood-stained coat for a robe of right-standing before God.

Isaiah wrote, "For he has clothed me with garments of salvation and arrayed me in a robe of his righteousness" (Isa. 61:10). Clothing, spun on heavenly spindles, woven on celestial looms, far more costly than our earthly budget allows. They could only be purchased with the life of Christ.

Turns out, it's a pretty miraculous journey from pit to prison to praise. Personally, I wouldn't want to miss it. Join me?

TRAVELING MERCY
Dear one,
You are worth every thread
Counted in your new garments,
And I personally
Designed and created
Your robes.
But you must choose
To wear them,
To put away your tattered and stained
Cloak and your prison wear.
My salvation,
My righteousness
Woven into a life,
Just perfect
For you.

NOTE TO SELF
What cloaks do I need to shed?

FORGETFUL

"It is because God has made me forget all my trouble
and all my father's household."

—GENESIS 41:51

We've all met people who pretended they had no past, no pain dragging around behind them, no troubles to speak of. Everything is always fine, great, good, super, no prob. (And don't we veer between impatience and envy, sort of in a "Get real!" and "Must be nice!" sense when we're with these people?) We've also met people who remember every single misdeed against them, who carry a long list of grievances against all who loved them less than perfectly. And then there are people so broken by their pain they scrape by without the tools or the will to chisel a sculpture from their stony story. They have never been able to move past the piercing wounds, never been able to staunch the blood and cleanse the gash of others' pain against them.

For all of these dear people, my heart breaks and I grieve. And for you and your past, for your pain. And my own. In some ways it would be easier to live in the denial of the first group, or the list-making of the second, or even in the sticking-place of the third group than to say with Joseph, "God has made me forget all my trouble and my father's household" (Gen. 41:51).

Some would give anything to forget their father's household, or their mother's, or friends'. Years ago a clever little lie surfaced, and Christians today brandish it like it's gospel truth: "Forgive and forget." As though that were possible. Unless we suffer from amnesia or unless our pain is so far buried that we can't access it, we aren't forgetting anything.

Forgiving, however, is another issue. It means to no longer hold others' actions against them. To free them from the hook of our judgment and the anvil of our punishment for their imperfection or cruelty or neglect. To release them from their debt to us, the repercussion we think we owe them for hurting us.

So for Joseph to name his son Manasseh? To have said at his birth, with such jubilance, "It is because God has made me forget all my trouble and all my father's household"? Clearly he didn't forget, but he refused to allow trouble to become his warden, locking him in the iron bars of his affliction. (*Trouble* in the Hebrew means "labor, toiling, misery, abuse, bitter labor, oppressive.")

He hadn't forgotten the past or buried it by the great River Nile (or De-Nile, as some call it). But with God's help, Joseph shook free from his past and God enabled him to move forward freely.

Though he lived in Egypt, worked and wed and had children in Egypt, Joseph retained his faith and released his past. The Bible says Manasseh's name "describes God's activity on behalf of Joseph, explaining in general the significance of his change of fortune. . . . The giving of this Hebrew name to his son shows that Joseph retained his heritage and faith; and it shows that a brighter future was in store for him" (Gen. 41:51 NET Bible note).

We, too, can remember and then release our past, moving toward the brighter future. The newborn baby in Joseph's arms reminds us.

TRAVELING MERCY
Dear one,
Let go.
The past is past,
And today leads to tomorrow,
A brighter tomorrow,
Born new for you,
For all.
You will remember the past,
But the pain will no longer own you.
Commit it to me.
Face forward.
You never know
What I will do
With where you've been
And where you're going next.

NOTE TO SELF
No denial here. Remember, release,
and walk forward.

DOUBLE FOR YOUR TROUBLE

"It is because God has made me fruitful in
the land of my suffering."

—GENESIS 41:52

Plenty happened during the years of plenty, before famine decimated the land. God gave Joseph a second son, Ephraim. His name sounds like a Hebrew term meaning "twice fruitful." The name Joseph chose summarizes the leader's understanding of his own journey, and speaks a vital life lesson: "God has made me fruitful in the land of my suffering" (Gen. 41:52). Fruitfulness in suffering is like planting a vegetable garden in a rock pile in a drought. Any growth happens by deliberate effort and care.

In Egypt Joseph recognized that bearing fruit was a choice only he could make for himself. He could idolize the suffering, moan and groan and woe-is-me the time away. Or he could hit the spiritual gym, develop his gifts and glean knowledge, then employ that learning and wisdom on a daily basis in his daily rounds, whether in high position or in prison. In this way, suffering becomes a gift not just for our own growth, but also a gift to others.

When Cardinal Joseph Bernadin in Chicago received treatment care for pancreatic cancer, rather than entering the doctor's office privately through the side door, he walked through the front door. He waited in the waiting room with the rest of the patients. Maybe God would use this time in his life to bless others as he shared the commonality of pain and suffering. Perhaps he might offer comfort and hope to his fellow sufferers, because he knew the Source of hope. Of his journey with cancer, he said, "I have a whole new ministry since I became ill, and I am deeply grateful for that."[1] He, like the biblical Joseph, saw the suffering as an opportunity to bear fruit.

But a teeny part of me argues: Joseph was a big deal leader, one of the founders of Judaism. And Cardinal Bernadin was a big leader, too. They both probably had an inside line to God, probably had a teacher's pet advantage over the rest of us who just scrape by day after day, our backs bowed by difficulty and hearts heaving with pain.

Then again, Scripture is pretty straightforward about Joseph's trials, and the trials of just about everyone who chose to follow and trust God for fruit in suffering. Hebrews tells us that the mighty women and men of old were tortured, refusing to be released, facing jeers, flogging, chains, and imprisonment. "They were put to death by stoning; they were sawed in two, they were killed by the sword. They went about in sheepskins and goatskins, destitute, persecuted and mistreated—the world was not worthy of them" (Heb. 11:37–38).

In the middle of that passage about their suffering lies a critical truth: Their "weakness was turned to strength" (Heb. 11:34). And after listing all of his own sufferings, didn't Paul quote God's words to him, "My grace is sufficient for you, for my power is made perfect in weakness" (2 Cor. 12:9)?

Perhaps that was Joseph's secret, and Cardinal Bernadin's, a secret that can be yours and mine. God can make us twice fruitful—double for our trouble—in the land of our suffering, because God's grace overflows for us in our weakness.

What a bargain. What a bonus. What a blessing.

TRAVELING MERCY
Dear one,
Fruitful
Not once,
But twice.
Double the fruit
For all your struggle
And trouble.
I will turn your weakness
To strength.
Just keep
Pointing your heart toward me,
And pin your hopes on the harvest—
Today's,
Tomorrow's,
And eternity's.

NOTE TO SELF
Trouble plants suffering, but God grows fruit.

NOTE
1. Henri Nouwen, *Sabbatical Journey: The Diary of His Final Year* (New York: Crossroad, 1998), 9.

SETTLE DOWN

"God has made me fruitful."

—GENESIS 41:52

Even with his name change, his royal clothes, and his clean-shaven face, Joseph kept his identity as a Hebrew, a son of Israel. The names of his sons reference his past and his true identity, even as they remind us of the suffering and affliction he experienced.

Still, Joseph put down roots in Egypt. "God has made me fruitful," Joseph said (Gen. 41:52). Good fruit needs decent roots. Many years later, when the Israelites would be in exile in Babylon, God would tell them to settle in, build houses, plant gardens, get married, bear children, and pray for the prosperity of the land of their captivity (see Jer. 29:4–7). Joseph's descendants modeled his lifestyle.

Joseph acclimated to Egypt, though without accepting their morals. He slaved away, so to speak, by serving the Egyptians and preserving them, their families, and their country for the future. Joseph's settling in allowed for the preservation of his own family line and the fulfillment of God's promises to his grandfather Abraham so many years before. Because Joseph invested in Egypt and saved the nation from famine, his entire family would one day settle in the land.

As the country around them prospered, so would the Israelites as they followed God's command to be fruitful and multiply. And when, many years and many descendants later, God called the exiles back to Israel, they would leave with such favor from God that they carried the riches of Egypt.

To settle into a new land requires trust, whether for Joseph or the Israelites or for you and me this week. Trust in God that the investment of time to settle and put down roots will not be wasted. Trust that we are where we're meant to be. Settling, in fact, is such a sign of trust that I'm embarrassed that I haven't finished unpacking after our move ten weeks ago!

However long we live in our current surroundings, God calls us to invest our energies. To commit to the work, the relationships, the environment, and the future in this place. To build into tomorrow by settling well into today.

Even if you haven't moved recently, settling into today still takes trust. Trust that the God who kept us through the night will keep us and those we love through the day. Trust that the strength for today will be sufficient for its tasks and troubles. That our personal resources, which quickly deplete, will be refilled constantly by the Holy Spirit.

Imagine Joseph, on his first day at work in the number two spot in Egypt. On his shoulders rested the future of the entire nation of Egypt. He didn't realize that the future of his own people, the people of Israel, a country yet unnamed, also bore down invisibly on him.

But Joseph didn't need to know that. All he needed to know was what Pharaoh affirmed of him, there in the throne room with all those magicians and yes-men: "Can we find anyone like this man, one in whom is the spirit of God?" No, indeed not. And further, "Since God has made all this known to you, there is no one so discerning and wise as you" (Gen. 41:38–39).

With God's wisdom and discernment, with God's Spirit filling him, Joseph could settle into his work with absolute confidence. He could trust God totally.

Like Joseph, we don't need to know everything that rests on our faithfulness. Even if today doesn't feel very dreamy, we just trust, fill our lungs with God, and settle into the right next moment, safe in our identity as God's beloved.

TRAVELING MERCY
Dear one,
Settle your fear,
Your doubts,
All your unknowns,
And trust me.
I have called you to today,
And I will be faithful to you today.
And that's all you need to know
To trust me
And settle down
Into the now.
Not yesterday or tomorrow.
Today will be enough.
And so will I.

NOTE TO SELF
Where do I trust today?

ENOUGH IN THE MIDST OF FAMINE

When the famine had spread over the whole country,
Joseph opened all the storehouses.

—GENESIS 41:56

Joseph ordered all of Egypt to bring a 20 percent tithe of all produce to the storehouses. Twenty percent of plenty is plenty of grain and goods, and Joseph carefully documented every ounce. But the crops grew so plentiful that the storage units overflowed. With food everywhere, no doubt people wondered if Joseph's decrees were a little too strict.

With such bounty, Joseph stopped measuring and stopped counting. Counting just about always gets me in trouble. When I start counting, I stop trusting. Not to say that tallies are bad. Knowing what's in the bank is a good idea. But sometimes I count in order to see if we'll be OK. Will there be enough to get through, will the storehouses be sufficient, and can we cover expenses?

The 20 percent kept coming in. Joseph knew the country would survive with careful management when the famine devoured the land.

That's not the situation for my family, and likely not , either. We don't have enough funds or grains or other goods stashed away to see us through the year, let alone seven terrible, awful, bad years. It wouldn't take long to count and realize, "Whoa, we are in trouble."

Look again at Joseph, who stored away all the grain for all the people. When the famine reached severe stages and people began to starve, he opened up all the storehouses for them. Isn't this like God? When I count, I fear. Whether it's money, love, energy, emotion, or strength, we all count and often come up shortchanged in our own accounting. But there is an antidote to our fear. God commands us, *commands* us, "'Bring the whole tithe into the storehouse, that there may be food in my house. Test me in this,' says the LORD Almighty, 'and see if I will not throw open the floodgates of heaven and pour out so much blessing that there will not be room enough to store it'" (Mal. 3:10). We bring the whole tithe into God's storehouse, providing for the needs of God's house, and what does God do? He throws open the floodgates and pours out rivers, avalanches, of blessing. Blessings running over so big we can't count and don't need to count.

The faith required to bring a tithe (and most Christian practices hope for a 10 percent tithe, not 20 percent) is substantial in times of scarcity and plenty. And it sounds like a get-rich-quick scheme, some health-and-wealth formula: Give and you'll get back. But God says, "Test me now in this." Test God? "Test my plenty, test my faithfulness, test out the tithe-and-trust formula. Go ahead, I dare you," God says. The people of Egypt tithed their 20 percent, trusting their leader to see them through the coming famine.

Maybe it's time to stop counting and start trusting. To bring the tithe into the house of God and then watch for how God blesses. Blessing us that we might be a blessing. It's God's promise, starting in Genesis and running clear through to Malachi. Imagine. The church becomes a clearinghouse for the blessings of God, distributed freely throughout the world. Blessing, running over, spilling through our fingers and out into the world.

TRAVELING MERCY
Dear one,
Test me now.
Count on me,
Count your blessings,
Count on my faithfulness
As you bring your gifts,
Your tithes of time, talent, and treasure
Into my house.
My promise to Abraham
And through Malachi
To you
Remains the same.
Trust me.
Test me.
I will bless you
That you might be a blessing.
And also, I define blessing.

NOTE TO SELF
Stop counting. Start trusting. So help me, God.

YEARS OF PLENTY, YEARS OF LEAN

The famine was severe everywhere.

—GENESIS 41:57

We seem to have found ourselves in a season of lean, like Egypt in the days of famine. Last week, I did the math and realized that we have never gone this long without a real paycheck. And that, unless something happened quickly, we would be bankrupt and with soaring credit card debt.

My husband mentioned, kindly, that God has never failed us yet. I buried my face in my hands. "I wish that comforted me right now." He whistled a few bars to a tune about God's faithfulness. I bent over in my chair, moaning.

Sometimes I can't see through the doubt and despair. I want to remember that God has been faithful in the past. I want to remember that so far, so good, though also, so hard, so often. But the facts seem outlandishly larger than my puny faith, and I just want off the boat with its disintegrating cardboard rudder and no engine with only our arms for paddles.

We aren't destitute. Not yet. And God hasn't failed us. Not yet. (Not ever, but I am living one day at a time. And also, God's definition of provision varies wildly.)

Last week, I sorted envelopes on my desk—unopened medical bills and the final gas bill from before our recent move. Each one I opened proclaimed debt, debt, and more debt. The drum of fear rattled its hollow tone within me.

Well, what to do? I started calling the offices to make modest payments. The first office asked for our account number. "Hmmm," she said. "We show a zero balance." I clarified the amount due on the bill. "No. We show you've paid it off."

"It's a miracle," I shouted to her. "You've made my day." She laughed a large, rolling laugh, and the drum subsided.

But the pretty big pile of bills begged for resolution, so I called to make a payment on another. "Well," she said, "You don't owe anything. It's paid off." I clarified the amount due on our bill. "Nope. You're clear here."

"Hallelujah!" My voice trembled over this one.

The next call, the same response. "You've paid this in full."

And the next. By the time I worked through my stack, we owed money on only two accounts. Not counting the gas bill. That one still displayed a large amount after our brutal winter. I called to see about payments. "What's your account number again?" the man asked. I repeated it. "What address is it again?" I repeated it. "Wait, what phone number is associated with the account?"

I waited, hoping we could make payments. Leaving our last home took every spare cent.

"Ma'am," he said. "Looks like you owe $12.12."

My heart about stopped. Then I started laughing. "Twelve dollars? Twelve cents?"

"Yes, ma'am."

Should I laugh, or cry? Instead, I said, "This is a miracle. Thank you. God bless you so much."

I settled back into my office chair, speechless. It was impossible for me to resurrect the worry and fear. Bill after bill marked "paid in full" splayed out before me on the desk. It felt like Egypt in the years of lean—miraculous, God pulling grain out of the storehouse for us personally.

I know, I know. The mail waits for no woman, and there will be more bills and more needs. But I know this too: There is grain in the storehouse. God's storehouse, even if not in my own.

TRAVELING MERCY
Dear one,
Years of scrawny
Don't scare me,
So trust me.
See about my work,
And I will see about yours.
I will provide for you.
Trust me,
Even when the facts
Seem bigger than faith.
Stop wasting time worrying
About lean.
I am the God who provides,
Feast or famine.
Always
Feast on me.

NOTE TO SELF
Choose feasting in the presence of fear.

GOOD MEASURE

"Give, and it will be given to you."

—LUKE 6:38

Linda (not her real name) married the love of her life, and God gave them beautiful daughters. Then after a failed back surgery, her husband became addicted to painkillers and moved on a fast track from prescription drugs to the street variety. Heroin became his best friend, and chaos and fear the unwelcome new roommate in the home.

Linda shifted from a stay-at-home mother with a brand-new license to sell real estate to a broker at a time when mortgage interest rates were an outrageous 18 percent. The firm she joined shrugged their collective shoulders and basically said, "Good luck with that." But without income, her children would starve, and she would lose the house.

She drove to work the first day, overwhelmed by her situation but certain that the God she'd always trusted would provide for her and her daughters. In the car that morning, she also made a radical decision of trust. She had nothing anyway. She couldn't pay her bills and had very little of material worth to lose except the house. As Linda contemplated the principle of tithing, she started to laugh. "Only 10 percent? Why, that's nothing. Ten percent of nothing is nothing. I'm giving God 20 percent." And she headed into work.

She was the only realtor in that office to sell any houses over the next months, and with absolute glee she danced through, sending God the firstfruits of the income.

She has started over from zilch twice due to medical bills and her husband's abuse of money, but she's never missed a bill payment. She's never gone hungry. Her children grew up to love and serve the Lord, and before her husband died, God woke him from a coma and Linda led him back to the Lord. His entire extended family witnessed the dramatic change in this man they'd feared and avoided for years. And then he went to heaven. Talk about fruit.

And Linda? She is one of the most vibrant and dynamic women I've met. Her faith tops the charts, as does her energy and her laughter. She delights to serve and loves her work. In the fiercely competitive real estate environment, she mentors new brokers, teaching them everything she knows. Her generosity knows no limits. She oversees women's ministry and has helped many women learn healthy boundaries within addictive relationships. Not only has God not wasted her past sufferings, but God has made her fruitful in the land of her affliction. That, and a warehouse overflowing with joy. An impressive return on investment.

Maybe that's all part of the Joseph 20 Percent Principle: Give with joy and God blesses. Second Corinthians 9:7 tells us, "Each of you should give what you have decided in your heart to give, not reluctantly or under compulsion, for God loves a cheerful giver." *Cheerful* is sometimes translated as "hilarious." The background for Linda's cheer? Her pastoral leadership started the practice years ago. At the announcement of the offering, someone in the congregation let out a whoop and a cheer, and people began to applaud God. The more they applauded, the deeper they found their pockets, and the deeper their faith.

Jesus, nearly two thousand years after Joseph, said, "Give, and it will be given to you. A good measure, pressed down, shaken together and running over, will be poured into your lap. For with the measure you use, it will be measured to you" (Luke 6:38). If the only benefit Linda received was joy—oh, and effective ministry and also her husband's salvation and also her testimony of faith to her kids—well, that's plenty of blessing. Joyful in, joyful out. Now that's something to cheer about.

TRAVELING MERCY

Dear one,
I love your laugh.
I love you.
I love you when you trust me
Enough to give me your heart
And soul,
And your fear, too.
I will watch over you,
And when you give to me,
I promise to give back
Beyond anything you can imagine.
Give back.
Give forward.
And get your lap ready,
And your laugh, too.
We will laugh
All the way to heaven.

NOTE TO SELF

Blessed to give.

FINDING FOOD

"Why do you just keep looking at each other?"
—GENESIS 42:1

The widespread starvation ate its way to the house of Israel, where ancient memories resurrected. No doubt Jacob remembered the famine of his earlier years, which led his family to Abimelek. That led to the debacle of his father turning his mother over to the king rather than claim her as his wife. He probably remembered, too, that at that time, the Lord had appeared to his father Isaac, who, like Grandpa Abraham before him, wanted to hotfoot it to Egypt for food during the famine. God redirected Isaac that time, however, saying, "Do not go down to Egypt; live in the land where I tell you to live. Stay in this land for a while" (Gen. 26:2–3). Years before, Abraham had gone to Egypt without consulting God, but Isaac had stayed. Then after Jacob fled to the north for a long sojourn, he returned and stayed in the land of his forefathers. The land now once again in the grips of starvation.

"Stay for a while," God had said to Isaac. How long is a while? Now, his son Jacob neared 130 years of age. With the third famine in full swing, all the world felt its destructive forces. Terror and death would encroach from all sides, because without food, death wouldn't be far behind.

Then the good news of real food traveled to Canaan, where Jacob and sons and the entire family languished. Jacob caught wind of the grain in Egypt and prodded his boys. "Why do you just keep looking at each other? . . . I have heard that there is grain in Egypt. Go down there and buy some for us, so that we may live and not die" (Gen. 42:1–2).

If food existed in Egypt, then his boys needed to rush down there and provide for the family. With no herds to barter, Jacob sent off the ten eldest with silver to trade for grain. But he kept Benjamin by his side, not wanting to risk losing the only surviving child of his beloved wife Rachel.

"Do what you can to live and not die," he said.

It's good advice, then and now. What does *life* look like here, at this time in your life? How will you live right now? How will you find food, so that you might live and not die?

In various life and soul seasons, hunger manifests itself differently. Hunger for space, for solitude, for relationship, for mentoring, for friends. Hunger for Scripture, for God's presence. Hunger for involvement in meaningful ways, whether in the community or the church.

Whatever form hunger assumes, we need to take the hunger pains seriously. How do you recognize the hunger? And how do you satisfy it? Where do you look for soul food, and how often are you even aware that (a) you are hungry, and (b) you need to look in the right places for sustenance?

We can't just sit around looking at one another, hoping someone else solves our hunger problem and force-feeds us.

God has promised to feed us. But we must choose to live and not die.

TRAVELING MERCY

Dear one,
There is food
For your soul,
So run to me
And I will feed you.
Recognize your hunger
And your pain,
And bring them both to me.
I will satisfy your longings
In ways you couldn't dream,
But you must choose
To honor the hunger
And live.

NOTE TO SELF

Find food. Choose to live and not die.

CONNECTING YESTERDAY TO TODAY

"Surely we are being punished because of our brother."

—GENESIS 42:21

What did Joseph think, when his brothers bowed and scraped and begged their way into his office? How did Joseph get through that interview, except for God's grace and the training he received on the job as a slave/servant/prisoner/world leader? Even though he couldn't hide behind his beard, he'd learned how to mask his emotions.

For didn't those memories of their tortures engulf him? Didn't he relive in a flash the horror of being skinned of his clothes and pitched into the dark, narrow pit? And all those years of their taunting before that, weren't those crowding right onto the screen of his mind too?

Joseph recognized his brothers, the Scriptures tell us, and yet, as the scene unfolded, did he really? Because as Joseph observed them and listened in on their Hebrew conversation, he heard new sounds and attitudes. These men before him owned their sin against their brother: "Surely we are being punished because of our brother. We saw how distressed he was when he pleaded for his life, but we would not listen."

He saw them piece together their past lives and their present predicament: "That's why this distress has come upon us" (Gen. 42:21).

Reuben threw in his own observation. "Didn't I tell you not to sin against the boy? . . . Now we must give an accounting for his blood" (42:22).

Their sin would not leave them alone, and so it is for us. Sin will find us out. It's been true since the first generation of human beings. There are consequences for our broken behavior, and those brothers were absolutely right that they would not have been in that distress had they acted differently. In fact, they probably would have all been dead; the famine would have killed them because Joseph would have died and he wouldn't, by his careful planning, have been able to save the countries from perishing. This is not to justify their deplorable actions and attitudes, but rather to observe such a miracle that God took the sin and shame of that strip-and-pit experience and saved nations with it.

So Joseph remembered who they were, and then witnessed who they were becoming. And that is a fine example of distress working its way into character. They at last connected the dots of their past to arrive at the present. It's good work and vital for us all.

But Joseph also witnessed another deep truth. His brothers' personal inventory wasn't displayed for his benefit; it was for their own processing and would gain them nothing in terms of favor from this unknown leader. They demonstrated repentance in Joseph's presence without knowing he understood Hebrew or that he was in fact the long-gone, assumed-to-be-dead brother.

Repentance because of necessity. And when might genuine repentance be unnecessary? Never; genuine repentance is always necessary because otherwise our past continues to rupture into our present, creating a soul-barrenness not unlike a land in famine. Yet another way to connect the dots and begin to see the picture they form. Except, the sooner the better.

TRAVELING MERCY

Dear one,
Whether others know you or not,
Recognize you from their past
Or from your present behavior,
I know you,
And your past is history
Once you bring it to me
And clear the air.
I will always understand your language
And listen.
But don't wait,
And don't forget to take that repentance
To the ones you've wounded
So your past no longer hinders your present.
Go ahead.
Connect the dots.
They'll lead to me
And to community
And to your future.

NOTE TO SELF

Repentance leads forward.

DESERT REACTIONS

"I have loved you with an everlasting love.
I have drawn you with unfailing kindness."

—JEREMIAH 31:3

Just as the brothers' past and poor desert reactions pressed upon them in their current dire straits, so it was with this woman waiting in line to talk with me. Tears streamed down her face, and I held her while she wept. Finally she pushed her hair from her forehead and said, a sob still trembling through her words, "My husband left me. And now I have sinned in this desert place."

Thinking to hurt her husband for hurting her, she instead hurt herself and others by her actions. We can moralize that two wrongs don't make a right, that rebound sin is still sin. All that is true. But her desert reaction to the pain in her life, to the abandonment that left her high and dry in the desert, makes complete sense, though it damaged her soul and her relationships immensely.

King David, ancestor of our Lord Jesus and a revered role model in the Scriptures, was no stranger to the damage his own sin reaped on relationships. He said in Psalm 25:6–7, "Remember, LORD, your great mercy and love, for they are from of old. Remember not the sins of my youth and my rebellious ways; according to your love remember me, for you, LORD, are good."

Remember and remember not. David asked God to remember *not*, to leapfrog from David's sin to what is permanent and true—God's mercy and love from of old. To land on what *is*—God's love is his memory guide and God's goodness the measure. These are God's lenses for us in the desert. God's mercy, love, and goodness predate our sin, predate our desert reactions, predate entirely our wilderness and the resultant quest for freedom. These predate even our birth, for God is from "of old."

David was saying, "Remember who *you* are, God, and not who I have been, and bring me into freedom on that basis. On the basis of your character, not mine."

And we, too, remember who God is. When we recognize our desert reactions—the ways we have fought against the problems and pain that leaves its physical mark and the plain old sin that separates us from God and from our own hearts and from others—we are able to bring the soiled fruit to the foot of God in repentance. And repentance, someone once said, is changing the direction in which we are looking for love.

Most desert reactions, perhaps, are attempts to look for stability, for answers, for safety. But underlying those is an even deeper desire. We are in the desert, looking for love, without realizing that Love has brought us into the desert. And so we call to mind, to ours and to God's: "According to your love remember me. Not my sins, not my desert reactions. Remember me. Find me, God, in this vast and endless desert place, and love me, for you are of old."

TRAVELING MERCY
Dear one,
Will you look for my love
In the wilderness
Rather than hoping others
Will meet that need for you?
Will you wait with your desert reactions
And look for their deep taproot
That seeks a perfect safety
And a perfect love?
Look to me,
For I remember you,
And I remember I have loved you
From of old,
From the genesis of time.

NOTE TO SELF
Don't react. Wait and look to God's love.

THE HEART'S CRY

"You have deprived me of my children. . . .
Everything is against me."

—GENESIS 42:36

The brothers returned home, sacks filled with grain and minds with trepidation. This food would last only so long, and then they would have to fight their father to return. Back in Canaan, the family discovered the silver in the sacks of grain. This could only be trouble. Now they would be accused of thievery as well as bear the guilt of deserting Simeon, even while carrying the long-ago stain of their handling of Joseph.

Seeing the silver, Jacob blanched and assumed the worst for Simeon in prison. "You have deprived me of my children. Joseph is no more, and Simeon is no more, and now you want to take Benjamin. *Everything is against me*" (Gen. 42:36, emphasis added).

Imagine how the remaining brothers felt, after their trek to Egypt for food and the impossible bind placed on them: to return with Benji or starve to death. Granted, their past behavior had been far less than exemplary, but now they'd made the effort to save their family. What could the brothers have done differently in Egypt with the second-in-command's demand?

Still, aren't we right there with Jacob, with a wail of despair, "Everything is against me"? Life falls apart. We love and lose. People die too soon or in tragedy. How easy for faith to turn to despair, all our dreams slipping down the drainpipes of a disappointing and broken world. "Everything is against me," we cry—or feel, or shout, or swallow the words and choke back our tears and keep up the pretense.

Everything is against us. We have to admit that at times this soul cry emits from us as well, even though feelings aren't rational. Even though we know it isn't true—I mean, really, just count your blessings, name them one by one—and even though Jacob's approach overlooked the nine hearty sons in front of him and their tribe of offspring, even so, we make progress toward recovery by acknowledging how it feels. *Everything is against me*.

But if we stop there, we stop the momentum of God's work and we deny the rest of the truth. True, we feel bullied by life, like the unaccepted child on the playground, but Paul reminds us of the greater truth: "Who shall separate us from the love of Christ? Shall trouble or hardship or persecution or famine or nakedness or danger or sword? . . . . No, in all these things we are more than conquerors through him who loved us. For I am convinced that neither death nor life, neither angels nor demons, neither the present nor the future, nor any powers, neither height nor depth, nor anything else in all creation, will be able to separate us from the love of God that is in Christ Jesus our Lord" (Rom. 8:35, 37–39).

Nothing. Nothing. Nothing. Everything may feel like it's against us, but God is never against us. Nothing separates us from God. Though our hearts break, we listen to them and then comfort our hearts with the truth: None of this can divide us from God and God's love and God's presence with us. Whether we feel it or not, that is the absolute truth.

As we apply that comfort like a balm to our losses and pain, the wounds are soothed and we can be present to the people around us, and to the truth, and to the options before us. Like, finding food to feed our starving families. And trusting God with the rest of our loved ones, however awfully hard it is to trust.

TRAVELING MERCY
Dear one,
Everything isn't against you,
But it must feel like that,
You're so far from home,
So far from heaven,
And the earth so unlike
Heaven in so many ways.
But remember what is true
And even larger than your feelings
Of desertion, abandonment, pain, and loss:
Nothing, nothing, nothing
Will separate you from my love.
You can trust me
In spite of the pain.
That is the ultimate truth.

NOTE TO SELF
Feel. Turn. Trust again.

NO GUARANTEES

"My son will not go down there with you; his brother is
dead and he is the only one left."

—GENESIS 42:38

Occasionally factories post signs boasting some version of
"200 Accident Free Days!" I'm sure that gives people courage
and determination to keep up the safety record, though
whatever happened 201 days ago worries me a little. After too
much injury on the job due to dangerous or unsupervised
practices, in the 1970s the government mandated volumes of
safety requirements. The Occupational Safety and Health
Administration oversees extensive guidelines about safe
workplaces. (Thankfully, they don't inspect my office very
often.) After tragedies in other countries with entire factories
collapsing, killing and injuring hundreds of people, the US
regulations make sense.

But even with rules, accidents happen. Equipment fails,
people slip, scaffolds collapse. In reality, life is a risky business.

And Jacob learned that lesson. For all those early years,
he clung tightly to Joseph and Benjamin. He made no secret
of his favoritism, nor of his heartbreak when Joseph was
declared dead. Maybe, beneath his partiality, Jacob was afraid

to love anyone else. Rachel, dead. Joseph, dead. Maybe loving others wasn't safe.

For the next two decades, he mourned and clamped down harder on Benjamin. Jacob refused to send him to Egypt on the second survival mission for food, and that parental protectiveness very nearly cost the family their lives.

Who can blame Jacob for his fierce guarding of Benjamin, his final remaining tie to Rachel? He'd experienced the absolute worst fate possible: the death of his child. But Jacob's insistence that his youngest son be kept safe in his care overlooks the significant fact of life: it isn't safe. Demanding safety halts the process of living.

It also creates a fear-based approach to everyday life, which seems a little self-defeating if the object of life is, well . . . living. Fear corrodes families and closets off their gifts and talents because life makes no promises about the safe handling and use of those commodities. Exploring them offers the possibility of failure. Fear is a thief and a cheat, stealing the adrenaline rush of risk and success and the learning that results from disappointment. It cheats people out of the adventure of really living in the midst of uncertainty.

Life is a faith-based adventure with no waiver of liability or money-back guarantee. All the lawsuits in the world won't issue a refund on the risks of life.

Requiring safety stops us from trusting God, which hinders our involvement in God's work. The sooner we release our demands that life and loved ones be safe and under our control, the sooner we get to see God at work in ways we can neither imagine nor expect. Safety cannot be our only or even our primary motto. God's work must go on, in us and through us.

Our safety regulations hurt the people we seek to protect and deny them the kick of risk-taking and the surprising rush of God's strong hand in the unexpected and unavoidable trials en route. They're blocked from the growth that results from stretching beyond normal, from daring to shift from the tepid lane.

Jacob learned that to hold on to Benjamin meant dying. And letting go meant living, literally, as in, grain to eat. But also living internally, spiritually, and emotionally. Fear of loss kept him from living, but finally Jacob relaxed his grip, packed some savory gifts, and waved ten sons off to Egypt. He learned, at last, to let go and live.

TRAVELING MERCY
Dear one,
I never promised safety.
Life is a high-risk route.
In the middle of your unknowns
Know that the no-guarantee rule
Has a loophole.
I guarantee my presence
And the joy of really living.
And when you unclench your hands,
I will grab hold.
You'll see what it feels like
To be really alive
And to bring life
Wherever you travel.

NOTE TO SELF
Open hands, release, live.

PLAYING FAVORITES

"He is the only one left."

—GENESIS 42:38

How did those nine brothers feel, and Simeon too, stuck in the jail in Egypt? They risked life and limb going for grain. They've spent their entire lives serving on the family farm, taking care of the family's interests and working for their father, Jacob. And every day of their lives, they've lived with the message that they don't exist, they don't rank. Their father doesn't even consider them sons, evidently, for him to say that Benjamin "is the only one left" (Gen. 42:38).

Hello? Who are these other nine men surrounding you, Jacob? Who is the man in prison for your sake? Are you really that blinded by your obsession with these two sons, the sons of the deceased love of your life? Blind to the needs of the others in your family to be loved, appreciated, affirmed, and guided? Blind to their hopes, their hurts, their dreams?

Maybe your story reads like that of these brothers. On a scale of one to twelve, you rank nowhere unless it's below zero, a big negative number. You weren't the favored child, or you didn't exist in a parent's eyes. You simply didn't count.

Firstborn in a family of two children, Nancy spent years proving herself to her parents. Straight A's, salutatorian of her graduating class, self-supporting, scholarship to college. Her brother, also bright, was the only star in the entire family sky that Nancy's parents noticed. He received all the money he needed to look the part of jock at high school, and his parents paid his way to the best college. And behind the scenes, ever since they were young, he'd been abusing Nancy physically.

In another family, the petite daughter got all the attention. She was a cute little pixie of a child, and people adored looking at her. Her dance lessons, voice lessons, new clothes, and special favors were all due to her most-favored status. Her oldest sister was hard-working and smart. Her integrity was off the charts and her sense of justice strong. She refused to think badly of her parents, but when she left home to start her own life without their financial support, she recognized the sick family dynamics and gradually distanced herself from them.

If you've been the invisible child or the go-to child for blame, if you've never been able to measure up to others around you, stop listening to the lie that you are not enough. Here's what God says, and you might need to repeat it to yourself every five minutes for the next year or ten of your life: "Can a mother forget the infant at her breast, walk away from the baby she bore? But even if mothers forget, I'd never forget you—never. Look, I've written your names on the backs of my hands" (Isa. 49:15–16 MSG).

Your parents may forget you, forget you have feelings, forget you are special, forget you have gifts. But God never will. God never turns and walks away. Those pierced hands remind God every minute of every single day, "You are mine. I love you. You are precious in my sight."

God does not play favorites, so even if (or when) we look around and see people who sure seem to rank higher on the most-favored list, it's a lie. God shows no favoritism and in fact abhors and forbids it. "My brothers and sisters, believers in our glorious Lord Jesus Christ must not show favoritism. . . . If you show favoritism, you sin and are convicted by the law as lawbreakers" (James 2:1, 9).

Loving this side of heaven always comes out dressed in or disguised by our wounds and our past. Jacob perpetuated the favoritism he experienced from his own father. Maybe we can do the same: learning to love others with the perfect love God gives us.

TRAVELING MERCY
Dear one,
There is no such thing as perfect love,
Except of course my own.
Your experiences of being less than
Are real,
Because families are human
And love through their own wounds.
But I'm loving you wholly,
And my love is holy.
So learn from me.
As you are loved perfectly from heaven,
You will find yourself
Loving more and more
And better and better
On this earth.
Love heals,
And love is the only way people
Recognize me.

NOTE TO SELF
Expect perfect love only from above.

JUDAH REDEEMED

"If I do not bring him back to you . . .
I will bear the blame before you all my life."

—GENESIS 43:9

Judah wanted to save Joseph's life by selling him, which is a roundabout way of telling us that saving life wasn't his only motive. Though Judah's idea worked and ultimately led to saving the lives of their entire family and the people who would be called Israel, his involvement in the save-Joseph-by-selling-him affair tarnished his character.

His character improves some after a number of years, when he moved to Adullam and through mistakes and, OK, plain old sin ends up fathering a child with his daughter-in-law by accident. But Judah began to live up to his name, which means "God be praised," when he declared the pregnant Tamar more righteous than he. He owned his sin in failing to honor his word to her (though not for committing adultery with a supposed prostitute).

Still, there is room for improvement, and he continued to grow. His moral trajectory showed upward movement, which is what we hope for in all of us. Now, with Simeon stuck in an Egyptian jail and the grain sacks flat empty, Israel ordered the boys back to Egypt. He seemed to have forgotten the Egyptian leader's stipulation: bring Benjamin.

Israel refused to listen to Reuben's offer to provide secure return of the beloved only remaining son. Then Judah stepped between his father and certain starvation and offered his own reputation as a marker for his father. "If I do not bring him back to you . . . I will bear the blame before you all my life" (Gen. 43:9).

This could mean the end to any inheritance, the end of Judah's upcoming role as spiritual ancestor of the family — the end of his family line bearing the Messiah. It could be that serious for Judah to bear the blame the rest of his life. So for Judah to step into the middle of his father's doubt and his family's well-being with such potential jeopardies speaks to his increasing integrity.

So often some breakout sin becomes the sticking point for our reputation with others and ourselves. To see Judah grow beyond his past encourages me. I don't have to stay stuck in that mistake, that sin, that breakdown. God has a trajectory of growth for us all, and as we sometimes inch and sometimes leap along that line, we begin to become more than a mistake in our past. Through God's kindness and Christ's forgiveness, we no longer must "bear the blame" before God all of our lives.

We grow toward our future, toward the fulfillment of God's great plans through us. Judah has no idea how his own family will fulfill the great blessing of Abraham.

Nor do we know that in our own lives. But we do know that God's promises to Abraham, Isaac, and Jacob, and throughout the history of the Israelites, transfer to us by the life and death of Judah's grandson. We, children of Abraham, rather than stay locked in our past, can live into our future.

It's a dream come true.

TRAVELING MERCY
Dear one,
Don't let your past sin
Determine your present actions
Or your future.
Today,
Live into your new identity,
Live into tomorrow,
And all my dreams for you.
Break free,
And start growing.
It's not too late,
Child of Abraham.

NOTE TO SELF
Live into tomorrow by letting go of yesterday.

NO PLACE FOR PANIC

So the men . . . hurried down to Egypt.

—GENESIS 43:15

Panic nipped at their heels. People were dying without food, so the brothers hustled through the desert to reach Egypt. Hunger and fear dogged their steps. What if their father died while they were gone? What about their wives and children? And what about Benjamin? Judah placed his own future on the block to secure the travels of Benjamin, the other requisite Joseph gave them.

The future hinged on this junket to Egypt, where people ate in spite of a famine. Visions of storage bins overflowing with grain, fueled their resolve.

Running is easy when you're frightened, which the brothers surely were, but running hungry is a bad way to move through the desert in hopes of finding food at the end of the journey. Hurry too hard and you might die of heat stroke or simple exhaustion or, say, starvation.

A land in the grips of famine offered little in the way of food. No road stands, not even roadkill, because animals can't live without food and water either.

The journey of two or three hundred miles required desert wisdom. There are a few simple rules for desert hikes.

Pack light. Don't drag a bunch of excess weight. You'll be sorry and also sore.

Travel with companions. Hike alone and you're prey for problems: injury, hunger, bandits, wild animals, death. Hike together and at least you aren't alone in your misery; you'll have with others to bolster you in moments of fear or despair.

Capitalize on weather. Finding shade in the highest heat might spare you dehydration.

Bring water. Most people underestimate how much liquid their bodies and brains need to survive.

Bring food. Hiking takes energy; be sure to have fuel for your body.

Unfortunately, we sometimes hurry on our way and don't realize our next passage is desert. Spiritually speaking, it would be nice to enter all situations, every single day, with our tanks full of living water.

Using portable spiritual disciplines can keep the soul-well filled even though desert surrounds us. If we can still our frightened mind enough to listen, the silence might just reveal to us the truth of Psalm 46:10: "Be still and know that I am God." We are not God, but fear and panic drive us outside reason. We easily believe that we are on our own and the desert, since it's bigger than we are, will kill us. Except for the silence, panic will win and we will forget: God is God, both of the lush valleys and the barren wildernesses of our lives.

Feeding mind and soul with Scripture helps keep the emaciating qualities of fear at bay. Many years later, as Israel

returned to the Promised Land, Moses would say, "He humbled you, causing you to hunger and then feeding you with
manna . . . to teach you that man does not live on bread alone
but on every word that comes from the mouth of the LORD"
(Deut. 8:3). Feast on God's Word and soul hunger evaporates.

As for resting wisely in the desert? Wherever we find
ourselves, rest and pacing are lifesaving in good and hard
places. Can we trust God enough to rest on the way to the
next food station, whether an oasis or Egypt?

It just might save our lives.

TRAVELING MERCY

Dear one,
This journey from famine to feast
Requires desert travel,
But my food will sustain you.
Be wise,
Bring water,
Bring a friend,
And count on my sustenance.
Run on my power
Not your panic.
Trust me enough to rest
Along the way.
The journey is long,
But my grace is sufficient.

NOTE TO SELF

God's power, not my panic.

A SIGN OF LIFE

Deeply moved . . . Joseph hurried out and
looked for a place to weep.

—Genesis 43:30

They arrived at Joseph's office, grungy from travel, weak
from hunger, and quaking with fear. The silver in their sack,
double what they needed for their grain purchase, would repay
the ruler for the previous trip's grain. From the moment they
found the original silver back in their sacks after reaching
home, they were haunted by it.

Ushered to Joseph's house, their fear skyrocketed. Hospitality
never occurred to them; they imagined punishment, robbery,
or slavery. They tried to head off the attack by explaining to
the steward about the mysteriously returned silver.

Fear nosedived, replaced by wonder at the steward's answer:
"Don't be afraid. Your God, the God of your father, has given
you treasure in your sacks; I received your silver" (Gen. 43:23).

An Egyptian servant who knew about their God? More
than that, respected their God? And what did he mean? God
had given them the treasure?

And then Simeon stood before them, freed from prison!
Did they forget their hunger and fear, their exhaustion and

grief, to see his face again, to embrace him? What a reunion, filled with relief and gladness.

The leader returned for a noon meal, and the cleaned-up brothers presented their father's gifts from home. This generosity in a time of deep famine greatly affected Joseph. His first sight of Benjamin about disintegrated him. "God be gracious to you, my son," he said, then rushed from the room to weep.

Joseph weeping. From cistern to slavery, from serving to a cell, from dreaming to daring, Joseph's heart remained open. All the grandeur of Egypt, all the clothes and chariots and the wealthy political marriage changed nothing about Joseph's heart. He acted with wisdom and compassion. He trusted God so much that people recognized God's presence with him wherever he lived or served. We've witnessed his anger and fear. But we've never seen his tears.

Now we see, at last, what the years cost him. We see his heart as never before. His grief, his longing, his homesickness swell at the sight of the one brother he really trusted. There, before him, stood the expression of that long-ago innocence and hope. He wept. In private, granted, but he wept.

That well in his soul reserved for grief never drained, in spite of the years of pain, uncertainty, struggle, and humiliation. In spite of the challenge of an enormous job, a huge learning curve, and the busy and important life of an Egyptian leader. The sight of his beloved little brother broke the barriers of these twenty years, and he couldn't control himself.

Water will always find its route. It carves grand canyons, deep ravines, tiny tributaries, and lines down our cheeks when it at last finds its way to the surface of our soul. Tears remind us of the importance of relationships, of the vital role of grief in keeping us alive and in releasing any bitterness and pain. Tears remind us of our humanity, our vulnerability.

For all who consider tears to be weakness, that image of Joseph—one of the greatest world leaders to ever live—weeping burns a picture on the retina of our hearts that we can't miss. Tears keep us alive. Tears keep us human.

TRAVELING MERCY

Dear one,
If Joseph wept,
Tapped into his grief
And that reservoir of love
And longing,
Where are your tears?
How long has it been
Since weeping renewed your heart
Like rain revives plants?
Allow me to rehydrate
Your soul.
Don't be afraid to weep
Tears of joy,
Tears of fear,
Tears of loss.
Weeping is a sign of my compassion
For you,
In you,
And through you.

NOTE TO SELF

What has life cost me? Where are my tears?

GRANTING FAVOR

"[God] has sent me to proclaim freedom for the prisoners . . .
to proclaim the year of the Lord's favor."

—LUKE 4:18–19

From the beginning of Joseph's servitude, Scripture highlights God's presence with him numerous times. When Joseph slaved away for Potiphar, "the LORD was with Joseph" (Gen. 39:2). He advanced to the position of attendant, and "the LORD blessed the household of the Egyptian because of Joseph. The blessing of the LORD was on everything Potiphar had" (39:5). In Joseph's prison cell, "the LORD was with him; he showed him kindness and granted him favor in the eyes of the prison warden" (39:21). The warden lived carefree, worrying about nothing, because "the LORD was with Joseph and gave him success in whatever he did" (39:23).

Joseph attributed his moral conviction to God when he stood against Potiphar's wife's seduction. And he insisted that only God interpreted dreams, not Joseph himself.

As a result of Joseph's faithfulness, God's favor accompanied him throughout his tenure of service and leadership in Egypt. People recognized the presence of God in Joseph, and they responded by showing him favor.

I pray for this for my children, for my husband, for people in servant-leader positions: that God would grant them favor in the eyes of others. Whether it's employers, interviewers, friends, or colleagues, I ask God that people would display favor toward them.

But Joseph's presence with others also brought God's favor *to* them. Whether in a prison cell or throne room, Joseph conveyed God's kindness, and God blessed the people around Joseph—their households, their work environments, the entire country. Joseph filled up with God and spilled over with God, and God blessed.

That's a far broader prayer for others: that because of our presence in their lives and God's love for us, God would grant others favor. Rather than pulling down favor for ourselves, we ask God for favor for others.

For our own lives, rather than troll for favor for others and from others, we begin to love and serve more effectively. We can't control God's blessing, but as we act like blessings, we bring favor wherever we go. And we ask God to act as in Joseph's time.

May others recognize God in us, see God loving and serving as we love and serve, and begin to experience God's favor through us. It's the least we can do. After all, God has delivered us from sin and death and moved us from prison to praise, from servitude to children of the Most High God. God sends us, too—like Joseph before us, like the prophets, like Jesus— to proclaim the Lord's favor.

Others need to know that kind of favor. That kind of God. That kind of dream come true.

TRAVELING MERCY

Dear one,
As you pray for favor—
My favor on others,
My favor through you—
You will be blessed.
Have no doubt
That others will see my presence
In you and with you
And long for me
Because of you.
So pray for them.
I long to show them favor
That they, too,
Might be free.

NOTE TO SELF

Life and prayer, flavored with favor.

BEARING THE BLAME, RELEASING THE PAIN

"Please let your servant remain here as my
lord's slave in place of the boy."

—GENESIS 44:33

Silver cup in Benjamin's sack and eleven men got sacked. They might as well all go to jail. They couldn't go home, not without Benjamin. But Judah decided, in desperation, for one last try. He threw himself to the ground, and explained Israel's great grief and the stipulation about the youngest returning home or Judah bearing the blame.

Judah begged to speak. He bore his heart. He pleaded for his father's sake, for his family's sake, to allow everyone else to return. They couldn't explain the silver cup in Benjamin's bag of grain. But in spite of their innocence, Judah prostrated himself before this world power, the man towering proud and furious over them. Judah promised to bear the guilt and the punishment. Otherwise, "If my father . . . sees the boy isn't there, he will die" (Gen. 44:30–31).

And then Judah said, "Please let your servant remain here as my lord's slave in place of the boy, and let the boy return with his brothers. How can I go back . . . ? Do not let me see the misery that would come on my father" (44:33–34).

Judah stood in the gap for the family. Judah, willing to bear the blame. Judah, so like the One who would come so many years later, taking the guilt and punishment for our sin. Judah didn't know the future, but already he lived into his role as the spiritual leader of the family.

Evidently, the brothers passed Joseph's final test of integrity. Seeing Judah take on the responsibility for the entire clan of men, hearing his humility, and listening to his story of their father—Joseph held it together. But Judah's final plea shattered the rest of Joseph's reserve: "Do not let me see the misery that would come on my father" (44:34).

Clearing the room of all attendants, the viceroy of Egypt, impressive, muscled, and clothed in the robes of royalty, "wept so loudly that the Egyptians heard him, and Pharaoh's household heard about it" (45:2). Joseph, too, could stand no more misery. A lifetime of grief, tightly bundled, carefully controlled. Hidden from view, locked behind prison walls of servitude and success. It burst through all restraints. Grief, like water, will find its path.

When at last he could speak, he unveiled himself: "I am Joseph! Is my father still living?" (45:3). Imagine, all those years, longing for his father. All the power in the world—and he had it—doesn't compensate for not having your daddy.

Joseph's story is, in various ways, ours as well. Everyone carries disappointment and loss in relationship. While it might not have been as severe as Joseph's, we've all lived through abandonment and betrayal. Not well, perhaps, but we've lived. We've held on, managed. In many instances, the loss and grief cost us our dreams, or at least, some dreaming time. Now is the time to release it. To reckon with the loss, to consider our own deep reservoir of pain.

If this is your story, then find people who love you, who will hold you as you mourn, who will honor your pain and wait with you in the midst of its outpouring. Grief, like life, brings no guarantees of replacement, but God, your God, is still living. Your God still heals the brokenhearted. Seriously, this is God's specialty, putting us back together so that the wounds close and then seal tight with the love that never leaves.

TRAVELING MERCY
Dear one,
Perhaps you are Joseph,
Suffering losses
You've never considered,
Never acknowledged or felt.
Or Judah carrying another's pain
And bearing the blame.
Now is a good time
To unburden your soul
And allow me
To tie up those wounds.
I am, after all,
The Great Physician
With healing
In my wings.
And I always stand in the gap,
Waiting.

NOTE TO SELF
Open heart; find healing.

HARVESTING HOPE

"It was to save lives that God sent me ahead of you."

—Genesis 45:5

If their past hadn't haunted them enough before, it sure haunted them now. The brothers stared wide-eyed at the man before them. The man in his rich robes ruling the country and saving the world. The man with tears rolling down his cheeks, entirely undone. The man telling them right now, through choking sobs, "I am your brother Joseph" (Gen. 45:4).

They'd never seen anyone raised from the dead, but if it were possible, they'd have believed it then. Because there stood the man they'd considered dead for years. They'd last seen him stripped naked with iron around his neck and heavy shackles clanging at his ankles rubbing his young skin raw. They'd spent years trying to battle down the shame, beating away its flame of reproach. Years trying not to hear their brother's fear, that cry for help, the bewilderment in his teenaged eyes.

As one, their hearts plummeted to the cold floor below them. Their spirits sank like a bucket of rocks into an empty well. Then terror invaded. Joseph? *Joseph?* He could kill them all. He could torture them, sell them, shackle them.

But Joseph's voice interrupted. Joseph the wise, Joseph the commander, Joseph the . . . compassionate? They stared, unable to believe what they heard.

"Come close to me. . . . I am your brother Joseph, the one you sold into Egypt! And now, do not be distressed and do not be angry with yourselves for selling me here, because it was to save lives that God sent me ahead of you" (45:4–5).

Joseph's understanding of God's purposes reveals just how centered he'd been for all those years. His perspective reveals such deep faith in God, in God's active presence in spite of and in the middle of suffering.

He framed words for what we are afraid to hope: that suffering and evil will not be the undoing of the world. God will ultimately undo evil, perhaps long years ahead of us.

Joseph's words offer hope for all who've experienced evil from another, for all who've been disappointed in another's actions or nonactions, for anyone who lives with abandonment or loss. For all who suffer. God will bring good from evil. Without that hope, there is none.

But Joseph's response also offers hope to all of us who have hurt another. For any who carry corrosive shame over our sin against others, Joseph's words are the antidote. In spite of our sin, God will bring good. This doesn't free us from the need for repentance or transform a wrong into a right. It doesn't mean we can keep hurting others because God will always fix it.

Of course wounded people without healing turn and wound others. Surely the brothers acted out of their own brokenness and pain at being the lesser-than brothers, unloved by their father. Surely their evil actions grew from such pain. While this doesn't excuse their actions—and Joseph never does—it does foster understanding and healing.

But Joseph made a decision to grow from the wounds and give life, instead. And hope. Joseph did not cooperate with the evil through bitterness or further ugliness. He cooperated with God who wrings good from the worst of messes.

Because of that, there, in Egypt, in the midst of a famine, they feasted. A crop of hope. A roomful of grace. Twelve men, harvesting the miraculous.

TRAVELING MERCY
Dear one,
That can be your story, too,
A harvest of surprise,
A crop of hope.
The pain of the past
Can be changed to good.
Invite me into the pit, the problem, and the pain,
And let's have a go
At healing and harvest.
Don't waste the pain.
Don't waste any more time.
I will not allow another's evil
Against you
To win.
You are Joseph,
And I intend to bring good.

NOTE TO SELF
Growth changes past evil to future good.

A REAL FEAST

"You shall live in the region of Goshen, . . . I will provide
for you there, because five years of famine are still to come."

—GENESIS 45:10–11

When the brothers finished hugging and weeping, Joseph
again assumed leadership. The brothers would return home
immediately and bring Jacob to Egypt. Otherwise, the five
remaining years of famine would leave the family destitute.
Word spread to Pharaoh, who couldn't be more pleased that
Joseph reunited with his brothers. He, too, ordered the return
of the entire family.

In spite of the famine, the family would enjoy the riches
of the land. It's a challenge, in famine times, to learn to feast.

LeeAnn (not her real name) approached me after a ladies'
day. "I was anorexic as a young woman. It's taken me years
to realize that food is my friend, not my enemy. But today,
God convicted me that I have been starving myself spiritually.
I've been fasting in the wilderness." She began to cry. "And
it's killing me." Her famine of longing for God's Word, God's
presence, and God's love song over her.

Her story, as it turned out, was Joseph's sister Dinah's story.
Raped with a knife at her throat in her twenties, not eating was

her attempt to disappear, to obliterate the body that seemed to have brought down such shame on her. Since then, she'd worked toward healing, but not through her local church community. She revisited that devastation, the mishandling of her pain in an era when people did not understand how to help. An era of silence, of blank stares and shushing. And she began to listen, again, to her own story, and God writing in the pages of her life.

Since then, she turned off all background noise. Her life had gotten away from her, the activities running her ragged and wasting her. The noise drained her energy. So she simply turned it off. Silence when driving the car. Silence in the house—no television, no music. She tried to minimize the volume at work. The quiet led to deeper listening. Listening brought her into a new, spacious place. In silence she could hear her own soul again after years of outshouting her inner self. There she realized that in the silence, the internal soul fractures healed. Her anxiety level diminished dramatically. And her hunger for God increased in proportion.

She left our time a new woman. Lighthearted, moving toward freedom. Loved, healing, and telling her story. And full. Full of God. Emptying of tears. Full of laughter. Emptying of pain. Filling with hope that her journey not be wasted, but be an instrument of healing for others.

In that silence, she recognized the truth of Psalm 46:10: "Be still, and know that I am God." God over LeeAnn's life, God over her healing, and God over all the intersections yet to come. God who extracts good from the evil done to her.

God who leads from famine to feasting.

TRAVELING MERCY

Dear one,
Turn down the volume
Of all the voices in your life,
In your past,
In your present,
Inside you.
Only then can you begin
To listen deeply.
Silence heals.
Into that silence
I will speak
My love for you,
My hope for you,
My plans to nourish you
On the riches of the land.
Come to me,
You who are hungry,
And we will share
A feast.

NOTE TO SELF

Silence and listening: a double feasting.

WHERE ARE YOU?

When he reached Beersheba, he offered sacrifices
to the God of his father Isaac.

—GENESIS 46:1

Returning home, the brothers tumbled over themselves like puppies, telling Israel, "Joseph is alive! He lives!" Jacob's shock converted to action, joy and anticipation empowering him. He loaded all they possessed onto the carts Pharaoh provided. But Jacob's journey out of Canaan included one last vital stop.

Beersheba. The place of Abraham's treaty, where he planted a tamarisk tree and "called upon the name of the LORD, the Eternal God" (Gen. 21:33). There, Israel offered sacrifices to the God of his father, Isaac. And there, God spoke to him again in a vision at night, and said, "Jacob! Jacob!" (46:2).

God called him by his old name: Remember, Jacob. Remember who you were. Remember where you have been. Remember that you who were once the deceiver, the thief, the shyster, are now called God-wrestler. You are now called after me, "God fights for me."

God called. And Jacob answered, the answer of his father and his father before him: "Here I am" (46:2). Present, ready, willing. The same answer given by Joseph, when his own father called him to go check on the other brothers. Here I am, ready, present, waiting to obey. Here I am, all of me, for all of you.

"'I am God, the God of your father," [God] said. 'Do not be afraid to go down to Egypt, for I will make you into a great nation there. I will go down to Egypt with you, and I will surely bring you back again. And Joseph's own hand will close your eyes'" (Gen. 46:3–4).

Do not be afraid. God's word to Jacob is God's word to us today. Your dream isn't yet fulfilled, but, God says, "Do not be afraid." Why not? Fear is logical. Fear is warranted. Our circumstances so often are tailor-made for fear.

"Do not be afraid, because I . . ." God says. Do not be afraid because God goes with you. God is the one who leads. It is God who guides. It is God who promises to bring us back to the land of promise, to the fulfillment of the long-ago dream.

Do not be afraid. God goes with you. The beginning of the next phase of dream fulfillment, not just Joseph's but all the generations of Abraham before him, were just beginning.

So after hearing from God again, rejuvenated by this personal word from the God he'd worshiped throughout his life, Jacob left Beersheba. All his sons and their wives and all his grandchildren, carts and caravans of people and possessions. He practically danced his way down to Egypt, the chorus singing in his heart and soul, "My son was dead, yet he lives. I will live to see my son." It was too soon to die.

In spite of five more years of famine, the feasting began. Reunion, sweet reunion just ahead. "Jacob lived in Egypt seventeen years" (47:28), far from dead, very much alive. Content, surrounded by his family, heart full, rejoicing.

"Here I am," he said. And here we are. And here is God, saying, "Do not be afraid." And God is good. God is faithful. God will deliver us.

TRAVELING MERCY

Dear one,
Here I am,
And here you are,
And together we head
Into the dream,
Into the land of promise.
It might not look like a dream,
But I promise.
Do not be afraid;
I am with you
To deliver you
And to bring your dream
Into reality.
The only sacrifice I want
Is your very own,
"Here I am,
Ready, willing."
Let's go.

NOTE TO SELF

Where is the fear? Where is God?

FORWARDING THE BLESSING

"I am about to die, but God will be with you."

—Genesis 48:21

One hundred forty-seven years. Years that spanned countries, feasting, and famine. Years of rejoicing and mourning. Years of pain and laughter. Jacob's rich life waned, and Joseph brought his two sons, Manasseh and Ephraim, to see his father. Jacob sparked to life at the sight of Joseph.

And one generation spoke faith into the next. Jacob reminded Joseph of God Almighty's appearance long ago, and the promise to make Jacob fruitful, to multiply his numbers. He called Joseph to remember, God's words: "I will make you a community of peoples, and I will give this land as an everlasting possession to your descendants after you" (Gen. 48:4).

There on his sick bed, Jacob adopted the grandsons, Ephraim and Manasseh, reckoning them as his own. Then Jacob spotted the boys and called them to his side. "Bring them to me so I may bless them" (48:9). But his eyes. He could barely see, but he hugged and kissed his newly adopted sons.

Jacob blessed the boys, crisscrossed his hands on their heads, and offered a moving prayer over them, for guidance, for shepherding, for fruitfulness (48:15–16). He closed with words now repeated in Jewish homes around the world as a blessing over the sons: "May God make you like Ephraim and Manasseh" (48:20). May God bless you richly, increase you and make you fruitful and faithful.

Except . . . that he crossed his hands and then bestowed the second-born child with firstborn status. Israel overrode Joseph's protest at this family scene repeating itself, for hadn't Isaac done the same with Jacob, blessing him rather than Esau?

Israel overruled Joseph's displeasure and taught the boys a valuable lesson: No blessing envy allowed.

The bottom line for them, and for all of us is that we be fruitful and multiply. Just as Israel reminded Joseph of God's work in their family, so we become people who remind others of God's calling on us, of God's work in our lives and in the lives of our loved ones. God's work in this world. For only then does the faith crisscross generations.

Years later the Torah commanded the passing down of the accounts of God's active presence in the lives of the Israelites. The Jewish people became a storytelling people, sharing the stories when they worked in their homes and walked along the fields. They spoke of God wherever they hiked, wherever God led them, always telling the next generation of the faithfulness of this God, the one true God, the eternal God, God Almighty.

This is the same God who called a young man with a dream into the most frightening circumstances and then proved to be the strong God, mighty to save, powerful to deliver. The God who calls you, who calls me, into a dream. That we might be the people of God, people who pass on the stories of the one true God, the eternal God, God Almighty.

The God who delivers. A big dream. A big blessing. Forward blessing, all the way home.

TRAVELING MERCY
Dear one,
My dream for you,
Calling for you:
Tell the stories.
Tell my stories—
The wonders of a love
Bigger than life,
The miracle of identity,
You,
My child,
My treasure,
My heir,
My dream.
Be fruitful,
Multiply,
Bless.
And I will be with you.
Mighty to save.
Delighting in you.
Rejoicing over you
With singing.

NOTE TO SELF
Start the stories. Bless forward.

THE INHERITANCE

"Gather around so I can tell you what will happen
to you in days to come."

—GENESIS 49:1

The famine ends, fields green, sheep fatten. Happy. And then, amid this prospering scene in Goshen, Jacob calls the clan to his bedside. It is time to relay the inheritance. Twelve brothers, plus Ephraim and Manasseh now adopted as brothers. A lot of family, reunited, now gathered around their dying father, Israel.

And they have expectations. The firstborn son gets a windfall, really: the birthright of a double portion of the estate, in order to care for any widows or unmarried sisters as long as he lives. Then there's the spiritual leader, who is the executor of the estate, overseeing the inheritance and its distribution. In addition, this child tended to the entire family's spiritual care, reminding them of God's faithfulness. Reminding them to trust that the God who promised them their own land would deliver on that promise in due time. Reminding them to stay faithful. All the rest received equal shares of the estate.

But Jacob's coming blessing entailed more than simply material goods (especially since the family owned no land in

Canaan except a burial cave, and possibly the little lot outside Shechem). He would have been watching for a son who'd proven faithful in leadership and responsibility. And for a son who demonstrated the spiritual capacity required for the blessing. The inheritance would be carefully spoken, crafted specifically for each son's history and personality.

And that was a bit of a problem. Because the past returned to haunt them. Particularly those first three sons.

Take firstborn Reuben. Remember his hostile takeover statement against his father when he slept with Jacob's maid Bilhah (see Gen. 35:22)? Though called "excelling in honor, excelling in power," Reuben would no longer excel. No double-portion blessing for him.

About Simeon and Levi, who massacred the entire town of Shechem in vengeance, Jacob said, "Cursed be their anger, so fierce, and their fury, so cruel!" (49:7). They would be scattered among Jacob's other descendants. No double portion for them, either.

Because of their pasts, Reuben, Simeon, and Levi all lost the privileges of firstborn and next in line.

This sobers me as I consider my own past and my life today. All my own failings, some colossal and some small. Put this on a spiritual scale, and we have only one standard measure: Are we like God or not? Are we holy or not? Because holiness is the only guarantee of inheritance.

We are all Simeon and Levi with our bloody anger and hotheaded ways, whether or not we act on that anger as they did. Their loyalty to their sister, their outrage over the prince's treatment, is laudable. Its outworking was sin.

We are all Reuben with our infidelities, our subtle and not-at-all-subtle challenges to God's leadership and authority over us.

None of us deserve a single coin for an inheritance. We cannot earn it. We can't be good enough to accrue any blessing. Yet Jesus said, "Let the little children come to me, and do not hinder them, for the kingdom of heaven belongs to such as these" (Matt. 19:14). First Peter 1:1–5 speaks of the inheritance kept in heaven for us, an inheritance that can never perish, fade or spoil, all because of the One who would come and rescue us from the death of our lives and bring us from our deathbed of sin to a living hope in Christ Jesus.

Like the children of Israel who owned no land in the country of promise but who waited for the promise's fulfillment, so we, too, wait for our undeserved and much anticipated inheritance: the kingdom.

TRAVELING MERCY

Dear one,
Your inheritance
Is not one of silver and gold
Or valuable lands
Or heirlooms passed down
From the hands
Of people who love you,
But rather the unfading
And undeserved rights
Of a child of God
Secured for you
By my Child,
My very own
Firstborn Son.
I hold it for you
And secure it for you,
So hold on.
The best is yet to be seen.
Meanwhile,
Live in my full forgiveness,
And follow me.

NOTE TO SELF

Live toward the kingdom.

THE STORYLINE OF SUCCESS

"Gather around so I can tell you what will
happen to you in days to come."

—GENESIS 49:1

We love the idea of a teenage dream, especially one that shows such promise and personal potential and power. It's a bit heady, that dream business, to most of us with our humble lives and humble or even nonexistent dreams. And what's not to like about a gorgeous coat that singles us out as special, much loved, Daddy's favorite?

And maybe we're a wee bit envious of that dream of glory. And look at how it was fulfilled. We love the way the story ends: Joseph, a real rags-to-riches success story. A world leader who saves the world from famine and guarantees the continuation of the family line that brings the only Savior ever able to save the world from both sin and death. It's the stuff of smash-hit musicals and award-winning movies.

Jumping from dream and dream coat and dreamboat teen, high-jumping over the years leading up to the bowing down part, the scene where the hero gets his palace clothes and rides in a chariot with people calling out, "Make way"—well, that's not fair. It's also not honest or real.

Because the journey Joseph took from dream to fulfillment was not for the fainthearted. It required more than a dreamy look and savvy mind. Joseph endured more hardship in the first thirty years of his life than most of us in North America can imagine—and most of that hardship clustered in the formative years of seventeen through thirty.

Dreaming is a gift from God, and dream fulfillment is too. And the route requires a storehouse full of fortitude. The constant application of mind over matter, of faith in a God who is bigger and more reliable than the facts. Of determination over desperation.

Once Joseph felt the anguish of his brothers' violence and experienced the sting of the whip and the raw cut of those heavy metal shackles around his neck and ankles, after he paraded naked across the slave auction block, this young man made a decision. The ugliness en route to the dream would not be wasted. The dream's fulfillment became far more precious because of the difficulty, and his determination hardened. The flabby-souled youth became a man of spiritual muscle during his Egyptian workout.

How many times did he want to quit? How often did he, throughout a lifetime of both grandeur and grunt work, decide, "I'm done. I can't take this anymore"? He likely didn't harness the power of positivity every second of every day. He probably endured some dark moments, if not days and weeks.

We know for sure, however, that in spite of the darkness and the initial downward trajectory of his life, his character maintained a consistent upward arc. He held on to the God who never lets go.

It's the only way to the finish line, to the dream God dreams for us that we live forever together. Hold on to the God who never lets go, however pitted the path. Return again and again to the eternal light that burns in the pitch-black moments and seasons of our lives. We all have our cisterns, our damaged relationships, our prisons. No one gets out of this life without rattling over those routes.

In the long run of our lives, we too have a Joseph story. Because into the middle of our zig-zagged life graph swoops the God of our dreams, inviting us to be part of a top-ranked dream team with plenty of upward mobility.

Heaven. It will be worth every single moment of famine for the feasting around that table.

TRAVELING MERCY
Dear one,
Dream on.
Hold on.
Don't quit
Trusting me.
We're in this for the long haul
And the heavy haul.
But I'll never let go.
You've wanted to quit,
But instead
Feast on that certainty
In the famine of your fearful moments.
We're a forever team.

NOTE TO SELF
Dreams require determination over despair.

THE SCEPTER

"Judah, your brothers will praise you; your hand will
be on the neck of your enemies."

—Genesis 49:8

Reuben, Simeon, and Levi stood at the bedside, red-faced.
Maybe they were angry or ashamed. But they had surely been
cut to the quick by their father's words about their future. In
terms of birth order, then, we arrive at Judah next.

Here, Israel waxed eloquent, his words to become a stunning
prophesy to which prophets would refer and which priests
would honor for hundreds of years. Judah's brothers would
praise him and bow down to him. His hands would be on the
neck of his enemies, a deathblow, a vanquishing of all enemies.

Judah, fourth son of Jacob and Leah. Judah would receive
the blessing. Judah, a lion, his father called him. Israel said,
"The scepter will not depart from Judah, nor the ruler's staff
from between his feet" (Gen. 49:10). We recognize him!
This is the one for whom the Israelites would wait for two
thousand years. The Messiah, the one to whom every knee
will one day bow. "Your father's sons," Jacob said—all the
generations of humanity yet to be born—"will bow down to
you" (49:8).

Jacob looked forward to that eventual bowing down of all countries and humanity when he said, "Until he to whom [tribute] belongs shall come and the obedience of the nations shall be his" (49:10).

His blessing lands home with the miraculous hushing in our own souls. We recognize the long-term fulfillment of this spiritual blessing. From the New Testament, we know that the Lion of Judah, Christ, will destroy all "dominion, authority and power." Christ must "reign until he has put all his enemies under his feet." And then the great victory is that "the last enemy to be destroyed is death" (1 Cor. 15:24–26). What rejoicing! The death of death!

In John's final letter, he wrote, "Then one of the elders said to me, 'Do not weep! See, the Lion of the tribe of Judah, the Root of David, has triumphed'" (Rev. 5:5). The Lion of the tribe of Judah, the One who was and is and is to come has been found worthy to reign.

Who would guess this from the tribe of Judah? Judah, who abandoned his promise to his daughter-in-law. Judah, who sought a prostitute. Judah, who abandoned his brother at the side of a cistern. Judah, who demonstrated a lifelong curve of repentance, an upward sweep of responsibility. Judah, who displayed the heart of a mediator and stood in the gap for his family, willing to take the punishment for all his brothers in order for them to return to Israel with Benjamin. Judah, who chose enslavement in order to honor his promise to his father, lest he bring down his father's head in misery and sorrow. Oh, for the courage and fierce protectiveness of a lion. Oh, for a heart like Judah. For a heart like the Lion of Judah.

Dear Lion of Judah, hear our prayers. We bow our hearts before you. May your scepter never depart from our hearts. Rule us with your love, you who are worthy of all obedience and praise and honor and glory. Amen.

TRAVELING MERCY
Dear one,
I give you my heart,
Child of my heart.
Live into my love.
Live toward my love.
Become like Judah,
The Lion of Judah,
Every time
You stand in the gap.
Plead for another.
Put yourself
In another's shoes,
For their sake
And for mine.
And when you do,
You hasten
The kingdom,
You bring the rule
And Ruler
Of earth
And heaven.

NOTE TO SELF
Bring heaven with the Lion's heart.

A DOUBLING OF DELIGHT

"Instead of your shame you will receive a double portion,
and instead of disgrace you will rejoice in your inheritance."

—ISAIAH 61:7

Jacob's hand of blessing rested on Joseph, the dreamer, the one who rescued the family line. He inherited the double portion, the birthright. The same blessing that Esau sold for a bowl of stew to Jacob.

Joseph would be called a prince among his brothers. He would continue to grow in favor in Egypt, showing wisdom and discernment in all his agricultural and taxation practices, setting up an economy perfect for the burgeoning people group called the Israelites. Their tenure in Egypt would increase them to a population density capable of settling an entire country, and they would leave with the wealth of Egypt so carefully accrued through Joseph's leadership years prior.

The eleventh-born son would receive the birthright normally reserved for the firstborn, a double portion. And when we consider his life, and all that he accomplished, how easy to believe, "Of course, he deserved it." With the exception of Judah, we have little idea of his other brothers' spiritual or character development in the intervening years from envy to Egypt.

And that could be our story as well. We haven't proven to be as brilliant, determined, savvy, or discerning as Joseph. We haven't interpreted dreams and been handed the keys to the kingdom, given a chariot and royal robes and the king's signet ring. He deserved the double portion. He'd shown himself worthy. But we can never measure up to that level of accomplishment.

How easy to slip into the shame of our lack of achievement, our total undreaminess. We aren't Joseph. We aren't Judah. So where do we fit into this theme of dreams and blessing, of inheritance?

Shame, that soul-dogging sense of not-enoughness, the feeling that we are a mistake, a failure. A chronic sense of shame drags on us like cement shoes in a marathon, and aren't we exhausted?

Hear this, then, wounded soul. Hear what God predicts, many years down the road from Egypt and Joseph's double portion of birthright.

Isaiah prophesied of a time when "instead of your shame you will receive a double portion, and instead of disgrace you will rejoice in your inheritance. And so you will inherit a double portion in your land, and everlasting joy will be yours" (Isa. 61:7).

That is some sort of crazy trade-in. The stock market would go wild over this deal: trading in our shame for a double portion of God's blessing, an inheritance in heaven. In the times of Joseph and Judah, the men received the birthright and blessing. Not until many years later would women be included, in radical departure from that law, and then only if there were no male heirs.

Jesus appeared and opened his public ministry by citing the beginnings of Isaiah's prophecy (see Luke 4:14–21). He would astonish and infuriate the male hierarchy by including women in the blessings of God's favor. He would befriend the social and spiritual pariahs — the prostitutes, the destitute, the sick, and the demonized and demon-filled. All the not-enoughnesses that people the earth Jesus would invite into this astonishing offer: a double portion in exchange for their shame.

And Jesus would stand against the shame, strongly resisting it, on a lonely cross surrounded by mockers and abandoned by his heavenly Father (see Heb. 12:2), assuring forever the joy set before us by Isaiah.

Jew, Gentile, man, woman, young, old: double portions all around. The most amazing economy and inheritance. Surely we're dreaming.

TRAVELING MERCY

Dear one,
No more shame,
But a double portion
Of the inheritance,
Unfading,
Unspoiling,
Kept in heaven for you.
So trade in your shame.
You've outgrown it anyway.
You need to be fitted
In your garment of praise.

NOTE TO SELF

Meet me at the Shame Exchange.

THE BIGGEST DREAM

By faith Joseph, when his end was near, spoke about the exodus
of the Israelites from Egypt and gave instructions
concerning the burial of his bones.

—HEBREWS 11:22

When Joseph the dreamer neared the end of his life, God communicated another dream, a prophecy of things to come. God had been long silent in the records of Joseph's dream life. There was the double dream at his journey's beginning, from Canaan to Egypt. Here is the second recorded dream Joseph received: the people of Israel—and here they were first called Israelites—would return one day from Egypt to the land God promised.

This is the word Abram heard long before the birth of the man who would be called Israel, before the family included more than two people. Abraham's descendants would be strangers in a nation not their own and be enslaved and mistreated for four hundred years (see Gen. 15:13–16).

Israelites: "People who wrestle with God." But the word also means "God fights for them." God saved them in their wanderings through Canaan, back and forth to Egypt, and then as they remained in Egypt for a four-century stay. Aliens. Foreigners. Exiles. People without a homeland.

But dwelling as they were in Egypt's Goshen, they remained a set-apart people. And though without a home, they lived as people of the promise. People who carried forth God's pledge to Abraham: "Go . . . to the land I will show you. I will make you into a great nation and I will bless you; I will make your name great, and you will be a blessing. I will bless those who bless you" (12:1–3).

No doubt Abraham's family expected to become a great nation, secure in the land God promised them. But how could they dream of a troop of seventy men, their wives, and families, heading to Egypt to be saved from a seven-year famine and hanging out there for many thousands of days? And while there that they would multiply in number, becoming so fruitful that they threatened the ruling powers.

Even with the advance warning, they didn't plan on four hundred years of slavery. Not much of a route to a great big dream.

Then again, since when does God fulfill dreams in the ways we expect? God calls us and we respond, knowing that God holds all the cards. We make our plans; we try to be faithful. We hold on to the dream and build a team. And sometimes we wait. A long time. We can't always see the plans God has for us, but we learn to trust that God does indeed have plans and that they are good.

Joseph returned to his true homeland, the Promised Land, only twice. Once for a brief trip to mourn and bury his father Israel, and then, centuries after his death, when Moses carried his bones from Egypt to the family burial cave. Gone, but with a legacy very much alive.

And we, too, wait and trust. God's dream for us is the dream we want to live into. A dream, begun at the beginning, in the book of beginnings. A dream, sung over us from the heavenlies, that we might be a people who long for and follow God. A people loved in spite of their unfaithfulness, in spite of their failures. In spite of it all, a dream, dreamed by God, brought to fruition through a man named Abraham, with a son named Isaac, with a son named Jacob, with a son named Joseph. Joseph, who dared to dream.

Joseph, who would save the world from famine and save his family from extinction, and ultimately, through his faithfulness, save us all. For from his brother Judah, whom he saved, would come the Savior of the world. A dream only God could dream.

TRAVELING MERCY
Dear one,
Big dreams.
Big God.
Big plans.
Hold tight.
Love well.
Plan to bless.
I'm on your team.
You're on mine.
And together we'll build
A dream come true.
A world filled with people
Living to bless
And blessed to live.

NOTE TO SELF
Keep dreaming. God is big enough.

NOVEMBER 28

LAG-TIME LEARNING

His brothers came and threw themselves down before [Joseph].

—GENESIS 50:18

Dreams, fulfilled too soon, can be dangerous. The journey for Joseph from dream to reality required a time of servitude. Now the brothers bowed before him and pleaded for their lives, terrified that with their father dead, Joseph might hold a grudge. He might pay them back for all their wrongdoings against him.

Joseph must have flashed back to the years since his dream. Before his kidnapping and journey to Egypt, Joseph had scant experience bowing down to anyone. If he had come into any sort of power, then he might have been a dictator who insisted on subjugation. While in the Ishmaelites' caravan to Egypt, Joseph's feet were bruised in shackles and his neck was in irons (see Ps. 105:18). He went nowhere without permission, not with those chains.

During his lifelong layover in Egypt, Joseph spent years serving, first as a slave in an official's home and then serving in prison. But with those years of servitude, he learned the humility necessary to be a good leader. He chose to develop a servant's heart, growing through the most difficult season of his life.

Sometimes the lag time between dream and fulfillment is due to our own growth curve. We have much to learn en route to living our dreams, and serving others is one of the greatest means of growing into our best selves.

I worked in the dishroom in college, a decidedly unglamorous and even disgusting job at times, mucking around food slop and wiping equipment clean. It's good for what ails you and abolishes any diva attitudes one might hold.

My friends and I waited tables while in college and seminary and have never been sorry. I can clear dishes and wash them wherever I am, whether in Japan or Texas or the local church kitchen. I can still line plates clear up my arm and deliver them to people or balance a large tray on my shoulder. My mama, of course, taught me that gift of service, but busing and waiting tables honed the gift.

Servanthood never goes out of style. Jesus, the one who would come to earth centuries after Joseph, lived a servant's life all the way up to his death. During the evening, just before he was arrested, beaten, and dragged to the cross, Jesus served his followers. He loved them, washing their feet, and serving them the Passover meal, knowing that demonstrating love through serving is the only way people understand or believe it.

James 4:10 tells us, "Humble yourselves before the Lord, and he will lift you up." This internal bowing to God in reverence and in confession of our unworthiness translates into an external bowing, into gifts of service and sacrifice. It's Serving 101, and it lasts a lifetime.

Joseph's teenage dreams portrayed his brothers and his parents bowing down to him. In order for such a heady dream to be fulfilled, he needed to know how to bow down. He needed to have been in that humbling position himself. Thirteen years of service taught him to bow down, so that day when his eleven brothers humbled themselves on the floor before him, he knew exactly what they experienced.

Learn to serve. Yearn to serve. It's all part of the dream: God loving us and loving the world through our acts of loving service.

TRAVELING MERCY
Dear one,
Finding your dream
Involves losing your pride
And any attitude you carry
About your own superiority.
As you confess your sins
And bow before me,
You will learn to accept others
And serve them
Regardless of their seeming worth.
Learn,
Yearn,
Serve,
And watch your dream
Unfurl.

NOTE TO SELF
Practice my serve.

FORGIVEN AND FREE

"Don't be afraid. Am I in the place of God?"

—GENESIS 50:19

After Jacob's burial, Joseph's brothers were terrified that Joseph would hate and punish them. They sent him a message: "Your father left these instructions before he died: 'This is what you are to say to Joseph: I ask you to forgive your brothers the sins and the wrongs they committed in treating you so badly.' Now please forgive the sins of the servants of the God of your father" (Gen. 50:16–17).

Joseph wept.

His forgiveness was thorough. He accomplished his desert work. Not just the saving of many lives through wisdom during the seasons of shortage and of sufficiency. That would have been enough to celebrate and was significant desert work. But leaders who accomplish great things for the world and yet have ruined their personal relationships lose their integrity, and the respect of their loved ones. Their neglect or disinterest leaves a blight on the fields of their lives.

No, Joseph's work was more than saving a nation or two from famine. He saved a family from the cancer of unforgiveness, just as deadly an enemy of the soul as starvation is for the body. Bitterness and resentment are plagues, destroying relationships. The brothers feeling beholden to Joseph rather than freed by him would have led to destruction. Joseph wept to receive the message, such a broadcast of their fear. This is the first time we see the brothers' sorrow for their own sinful behavior verbalized. This is their roundabout confession and plea for forgiveness.

And Joseph wept.

He wept perhaps because they had again misjudged him for the seventeen years of their father's life in Egypt. They'd believed that Joseph's kindness was only due to the presence of Jacob, keeping a watchful eye over the family dynamics.

Perhaps he wept because for seventeen years he'd been overjoyed to be part of his brothers' lives again, to be accepted and loved, and here, it turns out, they'd been harboring fear. Their regret and shame so overwhelmed them that they couldn't recognize and receive Joseph's forgiveness. They'd lived without the full sense of God's love, salvation, and provision for them.

But I understand the brothers' anguish. Living in the reality of another's forgiveness for our wrongs against them involves deep trust. They appeared before Joseph, threw themselves down, and said, "We are your slaves" (50:18).

And how often do we fail to truly feel the inflooding tide of forgiveness, the broad delta of God's total release of our faults? How often do we fail to trust that the forgiveness is complete, that in fact God has been busy bringing about the salvation of lives in spite of our own sins? We, too, are slaves.

Today, wait for a minute. What doubts do you carry about the complete forgiveness from another, or from God? Where do you still wear the shackles of shame, its cuffs cutting into your soul and rubbing you raw? If you yet wait for forgiveness, reread Joseph's brokenhearted response to his brothers.

"Don't be afraid. Am I in the place of God? You intended to harm me, but God intended it for good to accomplish what is now being done, the saving of many lives. So then, don't be afraid. I will provide for you and your children" (50:19–21).

It is finished. Joseph—and then Christ—stamped "Pardoned" over the life sentence of sin. Because God saves lives. Freedom and salvation. Salvation and freedom. A dream come true.

TRAVELING MERCY

Dear one,
Do not be slaves any longer
To the sin of your past,
To the pain of your present,
To your doubts about
My forgiveness
And my ability
To bring good from bad.
It's my expertise.
But the best part
Is when you live
Into that freedom.
I save lives
So you can live free.
Your life sentence
Is hereby commuted.
Signed,
The God of the universe,
The creator of the world,
Your freedom specialist.

NOTE TO SELF

Today, I walk free by faith.

LAST WORDS

"I am about to die. But God will surely come to your aid."

—GENESIS 50:24

Joseph, a prince among his brothers. His obituary might have extolled the millions of lives he saved because of his perseverance through pain and persistence in going through pit and prison and palace in order to serve.

But the scriptural obit reads differently. Even as we know the impact of his life on humanity, we now see the depth of his heart. His family was more important to him than his work, than all the hours he worked, and than all the lives saved through his vision and sweat equity. His tears of reunion with his brothers, his tears over his father Jacob, his emotions on Jacob's deathbed as his father closed his eyes for the final time, and his tearful response to his brothers' final plea for forgiveness and restoration of relationship. These all speak of the heart of a great leader, the heart of a great man, the heart and soul of a great dream and dreamer.

Joseph lived one hundred ten years and "saw the third generation of Ephraim's children. Also the children of Makir son of Manasseh were placed at birth on Joseph's knees"

(Gen. 50:23). And his final words were words of faith: "God will surely come to your aid," he told his brothers. Twice.

Family. Relationships. A soul tender enough to show compassion, to weep, and to restore.

When it comes to eulogies, people remember not how much you earned, how many businesses you started, the long hours you worked, or how busy you were. They remember, instead, how you mattered to them, to others, to the world. How you loved and served.

How will your eulogy read? A good way to tackle a dream now is to look at the end result—a life well-lived and a lived-in life.

Dear friend, as we come to the close of Joseph's story, I realize that in fact the story never ends because it continues in you and me and our family throughout the world. A giant family tree, fruitful, multiplying, blessed to be a blessing. May we bear fruit, plant seeds, and bear more fruit until eternity comes to earth and we feast forever in God's presence at the Supper of the Lamb. Until that glorious day, we choose feast over famine. We choose forgiveness, growth, nurture, gratitude, and ever-increasing amounts of the love that never ends.

TRAVELING MERCY
Dear one,
In the blessing of Jacob over Joseph,
Hear this:
You are a fruitful vine,
A fruitful vine near a spring,
Whose branches climb over a wall.
Your bow remains steady,
Your arms limber,
Because of the hand of the mighty One of Jacob,
Because of the Shepherd,
The rock of Israel,
Because of your father's God
Who helps you,
Because of the Almighty
Who blesses you
With blessings of the skies above,
Blessings of the deep springs below.
May all these
Rest on your brow
O child of Abraham,
Child of God.

NOTE TO SELF
Begin at the end: My eulogy will read . . .

DREAM PRINCIPLES

From Joseph's Journey

1. If people are going to bow down to you, learn how to bow down.
2. If you expect people to bow down, give them a reason to look up to you.
3. If someone throws you in a pit, don't panic. Rescue may not look like what you expect.
4. We benefit from others' dreams.
5. Without dreams, we lose hope. Without hope, we disintegrate and lose our focus and perspective that life is bigger than we are.
6. Joseph's dream was less about him being the big cheese and more about sharing the cheese.
7. Dreams don't make you more special or smarter or more important than others. Handle people and dreams with care.
8. Be ready for a dream by maintaining good relationships.
9. Joseph's coat didn't help; don't put on airs.
10. Grieving lost dreams creates room for new dreams.

11. Treat others with care as though they, too, are Joseph.
12. Dysfunction hinders dreams.
13. Dream your own dreams rather than judge the dreams of others.
14. Dreaming is not the prerogative of only a few.
15. Threatened people belittle or silence others' dreams. Give others grace but not power.
16. Don't stop dreamers. Give grace for youthfulness and innocence.
17. Learn from the pits and prisons.
18. Learn from people who forget you.
19. Learn from those who toss you into a cistern.
20. Learn from people who try to use or accuse you.
21. Don't waste time hating.
22. Bring a plan to navigate problems.
23. Focus on the triumph not the trial.
24. Everywhere Joseph went, God blessed. Become a conduit of blessing. It's part of the dream.
25. Stand out as someone filled with God's presence.

ABOUT THE AUTHOR

Jane Rubietta's hundreds of articles about soul care and restoration have appeared in many periodicals, including *Today's Christian Woman*, *Virtue*, *Marriage Partnership*, *Just Between Us*, *Conversations Journal*, *Decision*, *Christian Reader*, *Indeed*, and *Christianity Today*. Some of her books include: *Finding Life*, *Finding the Messiah*, *Finding Your Promise*, *Finding Your Name*, *Quiet Places*, *Come Closer*, and *Grace Points*.

She is a dynamic, vulnerable, humorous speaker at conferences, retreats, and pulpits around the world. Jane particularly loves offering respite and soul care to people in leadership. She has worked with Christian leaders and laity in Japan, Mexico, the Philippines, Guatemala, Europe, the US, and Canada.

Jane's husband, Rich, is a pastor, award-winning music producer, and itinerant worship leader. They have three children and make their home surrounded by slightly overwhelming garden opportunities in the Midwest.

For more information about inviting Jane Rubietta to speak at a conference, retreat, or banquet, please contact her at:

Jane@JaneRubietta.com
www.JaneRubietta.com

From Darkness to Dawn—
the Birth of Our Savior

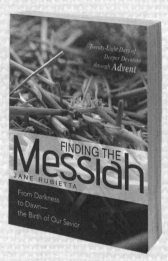

Through artfully told daily devotions, author Jane Rubietta leads readers along a twenty-eight day journey into the heart of Advent, in search of the living Messiah. Reaching past the holiday veneer of tradition, pageantry, and glitz, she draws readers far into the spiritual depths of Christmas, where Christ can be born again into souls. This deeper approach to devotion is still accessible reading for just five to ten minutes a day.

A free group leader's guide is available at
www.wphresources.com/findingthemessiah.

Finding the Messiah
ISBN: 978-0-89827-902-3
eBook: 978-0-89827-903-0

1.800.493.7539   wphstore.com

From Eden to Gethsemane— the Garden Restored

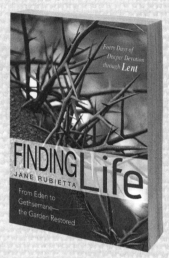

The life lost in Eden is found through Gethsemane. Follow author Jane Rubietta on her daily journey through the season of Lent as she traces the way that God the Son traverses with his people. Significantly, Jesus' ministry sometimes took place in garden settings: not only did he come because of what had been lost in Eden, but Jesus met with his disciples in a garden, he prayed in a garden, he was arrested violently in a garden, and he was buried in a garden tomb.

*A free group leader's guide is available at
www.wphresources.com/findinglife.*

Finding Life
ISBN: 978-0-89827-892-7
eBook: 978-0-89827-893-4

Finding Jesus in Every Season

Follow author Jane Rubietta on her daily journey through each season of the year to gain perspective, refresh your soul, and continue the journey. Tracing the lives of some of the Bible's greatest characters, these are transformational devotionals that encourage great depth. Walk through these stories from the Bible and experience life as these great characters did, gaining fresh faith and hope for your journey along the way.

A free group leader's guide is available for each devotional at www.wphresources.com.

Finding Your Promise
(spring)
ISBN: 978-0-89827-896-5
eBook: 978-0-89827-897-2

Finding Your Dream
(fall)
ISBN: 978-0-89827-900-9
eBook: 978-0-89827-901-6

Finding Your Name
(summer)
ISBN: 978-0-89827-898-9
eBook: 978-0-89827-899-6

Finding Your Way
(winter)
ISBN: 978-0-89827-894-1
eBook: 978-0-89827-895-8